THE EVERYDAY WOK COOKBOOK

THE EVERY DAY WOK COOK BOOK

LORNA YEE

PHOTOS BY KATHRYN BARNARD

SIMPLE AND SATISFYING MEALS FOR THE MOST VERSATILE PAN IN YOUR KITCHEN

SASQUATCH BOOKS
SEATTLE

Printed in China

Published by Sasquatch Books
17 16 15   9 8 7 6 5 4 3

Cover and interior photographs: Kathryn Barnard
Cover food styling: Julie Hopper
Interior food styling: Callie Meyer
Cover and interior design and composition: Alicia Nammacher / Sarah Plein

Library of Congress Cataloging-in-Publication Data is available.

ISBN-13: 978-1-57061-781-2

Sasquatch Books
1904 Third Avenue, Suite 710
Seattle, WA 98101
(206) 467-4300
www.sasquatchbooks.com
custserv@sasquatchbooks.com

To Weston, my sweet little boy.
Momma loves you and can't
wait to cook with you.

MON
TUES
WED
THURS
FRI
SAT
SUN

CONTENTS

RECIPE LIST

ACKNOWLEDGEMENTS

To the wonderful team at Sasquatch Books—particularly Susan Roxborough, Gary Luke, and Michelle Hope Anderson—I'd like to offer my sincere thanks for giving me the platform to share my favorite wok recipes. I never dreamed I would be able to have the opportunity to publish one cookbook, let alone two! Thank you also to Kathryn Barnard, Callie Meyer, and Julie Hopper, for their beautiful, meticulous work in styling my recipes. Your photographs translate my food so deliciously.

A special, heartfelt thank-you to my dear family, for supporting me while I juggled a demanding job, a major house remodel, and a first pregnancy while writing this cookbook. To my recipe testers—I could not have done this without your tireless commitment to cooking these recipes in different woks, on different stoves, to make sure they were just as tasty from my kitchen as from yours.

To my husband Henry, who gamely ate many a version of pulled pork, gumbo, coq au vin, and (his favorite!) kung pao chicken, and who bravely turned a blind eye to the dishes that piled up along the way. And last of all, to my new son Weston, who "cooked" along with me during the nine months it took to write this book.

INTRODUCTION

I remember my mom's old cast iron wok well—the one so worn from years of spatula-scraping that it has a deep indentation in the bottom, perfect for frying her famous little egg pockets filled with minced pork and fragrant scallions. That wok's patina is slick and black from decades of use, and oh, the dishes that were born out of it! Steamed whole fish with a smattering of ginger and a splash of hot soy, deep-fried sweet-and-sour prawns, braised eggplant stuffed with prawn paste, stir-fried pea vines with XO sauce—it's no wonder that the versatility of the wok, that humblest of cooking vessels, was instilled in me at a young age.

THE WOK

The wok was born out of necessity many centuries ago in China. Fuel shortages and frugality created a demand for a cooking vessel with a large cooking surface and a small base that extended the life of the week's ration of oil. It has been used for centuries in Asia; more intrepid Western cooks are now making this an inexpensive addition to their range of kitchen tools, and online availability has made woks much more accessible for the everyday cook.

As more and more home cooks are discovering, woks are amazingly versatile; they are capable of taking anyone beyond merely Asian cookery. With a wok, you can easily whip up a delicious chorizo hash for breakfast, fry up a plethora of goodies (fried chicken or homemade doughnuts, anyone?), sear a steak or steam some fish for supper, stir-fry vegetables or noodles for a quick meal, braise a pork shoulder for tacos, stir up a creamy risotto, or simmer a comforting beef stew on a wintry evening. Steamed custards and many British desserts (like the Sticky Toffee Pudding on page 128) can be made in a wok with minimal fuss. Don't have a double boiler to make your favorite lemon cream for cookies or cakes? This book shows you how to transform your wok into a makeshift double boiler—all you need is a tea towel and a couple of easy techniques!

Nowadays, the crossing of food cultures and the sharing of inspirations and traditions have left home cooks more eager to blur boundaries when putting together a meal. With a bit of creativity, you can make your wok the most well-used piece of equipment in your arsenal. Affordable, durable, versatile, and only getting better with age—it's no wonder that woks have been prized in the kitchen for centuries. I hope this collection of global recipes will inspire you to use your wok for everything from breakfast to dessert, and every delicious bite in between!

HOW TO CHOOSE A WOK

Woks are made nowadays with either a flat bottom or a curved bottom. Flat-bottomed woks are more suitable for home cooking (the flat bottom maximizes contact area with conventional stovetops and smooth-top ranges), whereas round-bottomed woks are used more frequently on high-powered restaurant gas stoves. I recommend cast iron or carbon steel woks over stainless steel ones, as the thinner stainless steel woks tend to not conduct heat as well.

When it comes to choosing a wok, a 14-inch or 18-inch size works best—any larger and you risk filling the wok with too much food to stir-fry, so it steams or braises instead. When stir-frying, it's always best to cook in smaller batches, so the food gets enough contact time with the wok. This contact time results in a sizzling seared surface that the Chinese call *wok hay*. Grace Young, one of the preeminent authorities on wok cooking, loosely translates this phrase to mean "breath of a wok"—that elusive seared taste of food that's cooked at a high temperature, which dissipates quickly as it cools.

My favorite wok to use at home is a hand-hammered carbon steel wok that my friend brought me from Shanghai—it's not quite as heavy as cast iron, but it has more heft than a stainless steel wok. When buying a wok, it's wise (though not 100 percent necessary) to purchase two—one for stir-frying and deep-frying, and one for steaming and braising. Many cooks do not like to steam or braise in the same wok they use for stir-frying, as the excess moisture can cause a seasoned wok to lose its lovely patina and naturally nonstick surface.

Though my favorite wok has two "drawer-pull," C-shaped handles, many cooks might prefer a wok with one straight pot-style handle and one C-shaped handle. This enables you to use one hand to flip cooked food onto a serving platter with greater ease if you so choose.

Two other optional pieces you might add to your tool kit are a bamboo wok brush, for removing small food particles when cleaning your wok, and a snug-fitting aluminum lid. The latter is helpful when steaming or braising—it accelerates the cooking process, and as you'll see, a number of the recipes in this book call for a covered wok. Both of these implements are readily found online or in the cooking section of your local Asian grocery store or the ethnic foods aisle of your supermarket.

HOW TO
SEASON A WOK

Before cooking with your wok for the first time, you must scrub its entire surface with a bit of soap, hot water, and a stainless steel pad. Wok purists will tell you that this is the last time your wok will be washed with soap—soap will strip off the seasoning that you've worked so hard to develop, and many cooks attest that a simple scrub with hot water is all you'll need to clean your wok after that initial scrub.

Once your new wok is clean and dry, you can proceed with either of the following methods.

SEASONING A WOK IN YOUR OVEN

This is my preferred method. It works well for woks without wooden handles. If you have a wok with wooden handles and still want to try seasoning in the oven, remove the handles, if possible, before proceeding.

Preheat the oven to 400 degrees F. Pour a tablespoon of vegetable oil, preferably peanut, into the bottom of the wok. (Room-temperature lard or bacon fat is also an excellent lubricator. The key is to avoid using oils with a low burning temperature, such as olive oil.) Using a clean towel, wipe the fat evenly over the entire cooking surface of the wok. Flip the wok over and use another tablespoon or so of fat to wipe its entire bottom surface.

Place the wok upside down in the oven and allow the fat to "bake" onto it for 20 minutes. Remove the wok from the oven to cool. Rub off the black residue that comes off the wok with a clean paper towel. Then repeat the process of rubbing down the entire inner and outer surface with fat (you'll need less and less fat with each round of seasoning), placing the wok back in the oven for 20 minutes to bake, and then cooling. Repeat these steps at least three times to begin developing a patina—the wok should turn mahogany or black by this point. If you have time, repeat this process five times to really get a leg up on your wok seasoning.

After this seasoning process, your wok will continue to season each time you cook with it. The pores of the wok love to absorb oil, so consider deep-frying with your new wok a few times or simply just frying your morning bacon and/or eggs in it. After each use, simply scrub the wok with a bamboo wok brush in hot water. Very soon your wok should become naturally nonstick, and you'll find yourself needing less and less oil to cook with in the years to come.

SEASONING A WOK ON YOUR STOVE

Place your clean, dry wok on the stovetop. Add a tablespoon of vegetable oil, preferably peanut, or lard to the wok. With a clean towel, rub the fat evenly into the entire cooking surface of the wok. Turn the heat up to high and heat the wok until the fat smokes. (Make sure to turn on your fan or open some windows to vent the smoke.)

Remove the wok from the heat to cool. Wipe out the excess oil—there will be black residue on your paper towel. Repeat this process—rubbing more clean fat evenly over the inside of the wok, heating it until it smokes, wiping out the residue, and then cooling the wok—at least three times. The wok will gradually blacken during this process and develop a tacky, slightly oily surface. Continue developing this patina each time you cook by deep-frying or stir-frying. (Some cooks swear by cooking up some diced bacon in the wok every few weeks just to encourage the wok's pores to absorb more fat.) After a few months of cooking, your wok should develop quite a patina, and you'll find yourself needing less and less oil when you cook.

Even an old wok can use reseasoning. If at any point you find food sticking to the wok's surface more often than you'd like, simply scrub out the wok with some kosher salt and hot water, using the bamboo wok brush. Then reseason the wok using one of the two methods just described.

With proper care and maintenance, your wok will soon be one of your most treasured kitchen tools. One of my friends has two woks she's been seasoning and cooking with over the years. Each wok is intended to be passed down to one of her two children, who are now only toddlers. She figures by the time they are grown and move out of the house, they'll each carry with them a beautiful, well-loved cooking vessel that's been tenderly cared for—one that's brought forth many a home-cooked meal and perhaps will serve the next generation in each of their new homes.

CHINESE PANTRY
PRIMER

Though this cookbook contains primarily non-Asian recipes, there remains a scattering of Chinese recipes largely inspired by my background, some of which are passed down from my mother and mother-in-law—two amazing cooks. Here's a quick primer to guide those who may be unfamiliar with some of the ingredients these recipes call for—everything listed should be easily found in your local Asian grocery store or the ethnic foods aisle of your supermarket. (For online ordering, AsianFoodGrocer .com is an excellent resource, as well as Amazon.com.)

ASIAN CHILI SAUCES
Examples include sriracha, sambal oelek, and Chinese chili garlic sauce—all delicious, and widely available where Asian ingredients are sold.

CHINESE SAUSAGE
Often vacuum-packed, these dried sausages are primarily made with pork and spices. They are a popular addition to dishes such as fried rice.

DRIED SHIITAKE MUSHROOMS
Often used in Chinese cooking, these mushrooms must be rehydrated in water until completely softened, before use. Dried shiitake mushrooms taste different from fresh shiitakes—earthier and slightly more pungent. They are used more often than fresh shiitakes in traditional Chinese cooking.

HOISIN SAUCE
This reddish-brown, viscous sauce is made from soybean paste, garlic, sugar, various spices, and a starch thickener. A popular sauce to enhance the flavor of meat, it is used for cooking, glazing, and dipping.

MISO
A thick, fermented paste made from barley, rice, and soybeans, used predominantly as a seasoning in Japanese cooking. When combined with dashi, this ingredient forms the base for miso soup.

OYSTER SAUCE
Primarily used in Cantonese cooking, this thick, dark brown sauce is made with oyster essence (or extract), a bit of sugar, salt, and cornstarch. Its savory flavor makes it a popular addition to recipes for chow mein and stir-fries or a sauce topping for certain dishes, like *gai lan* (Chinese broccoli).

SHAO-HSING WINE
This Chinese wine, made from fermented rice, is often used to marinate meats.

SOY SAUCE (DARK)
This soy sauce is often used for cooking, as opposed to dipping or finishing a dish. It has a slightly harsher, more molasses flavor than light soy sauce. You'll find that most Chinese recipes call for both light and dark soy sauce, as each brings unique characteristics to the finished dish.

SOY SAUCE (LIGHT)
Also called "thin soy sauce," this dark, flavorful liquid is made with the first pressing of fermented soy beans, water, and salt. Light soy sauce is used both for cooking and as a dipping condiment. It has a fresher, lighter flavor than dark soy sauce.

SZECHUAN PEPPERCORNS
These tiny brown peppercorns are used mainly in Szechuan cooking. They have a light, lemony flavor and produce an addictive tingling or numbing sensation in the mouth. To prepare for use, toast the pods lightly in a dry skillet and crush in your spice grinder.

BREAK
FAST+
BRUNCH

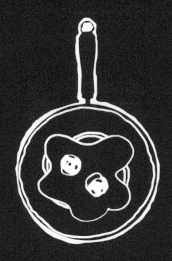

RECIPES

BANANAS FOSTER FRENCH TOAST

Those with a serious sweet tooth don't necessarily like to wait 'til after dinner for dessert. Luckily, now anyone can brighten their morning with an extra-special treat. This recipe features warm, caramel-y bananas spooned over golden-crusted slices of eggy brioche. It's a delicious take on a breakfast classic. Best of all, any leftover sauce can be drizzled over vanilla ice cream later!

SERVES 4

FOR THE FRENCH TOAST:
1 CUP WHOLE MILK
3 EGGS
1 TABLESPOON SUGAR
8 SLICES DAY-OLD BRIOCHE OR CHALLAH
VEGETABLE OIL FOR FRYING

FOR THE BANANAS FOSTER SAUCE:
¼ CUP (½ STICK) PLUS 2 TABLESPOONS
   UNSALTED BUTTER
1 CUP DARK BROWN SUGAR, PACKED
½ TEASPOON GROUND CINNAMON
¼ TEASPOON GROUND NUTMEG
¼ TEASPOON KOSHER SALT
¼ CUP RUM
2 BANANAS, SLICED INTO BITE-SIZE PIECES
VANILLA ICE CREAM (OPTIONAL)

Preheat the oven to 250 degrees F.

In a large mixing bowl, beat together the milk, eggs, and sugar. Soak each slice of brioche in the mixture, making sure the entire surface is submerged.

Heat 2 tablespoons of oil in a wok over medium-high heat, swirling it to evenly coat the cooking surface. Lay as many slices of bread in the wok as will fit. Fry until golden brown, about 3 minutes. Flip the slices and fry on the other side until golden brown, another 2 to 3 minutes. Transfer the French toast to a baking sheet and place in the preheated oven to keep warm as you fry the remaining bread.

Wipe the wok with a paper towel to remove any bread crumbs (careful—it may still be quite warm). Combine the butter, brown sugar, cinnamon, nutmeg, salt, and rum in the wok, and heat over medium heat, stirring until the sugar dissolves and the sauce thickens, about 5 minutes. Add the bananas and stir until well coated with the sauce.

To serve, place 2 slices of French toast on each plate and spoon the warm sauce over it; if you want to gild the lily, top with vanilla ice cream.

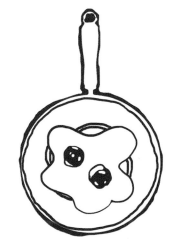

ASIAN-STYLE BBQ PORK SCRAMBLE WITH CORIANDER

Mix up your standard bacon-and-eggs breakfast with a slightly exotic scramble packed with chunks of Chinese barbecued pork, bean sprouts, fresh herbs, and shiitake mushrooms. The addition of soy sauce, sesame oil, and hoisin sauce makes this Eastern twist on an egg dish extra special—hold the ketchup.

SERVES 2

5 EGGS
1 TEASPOON LIGHT SOY SAUCE
2 TABLESPOONS FRESH CORIANDER
   (CILANTRO), FINELY CHOPPED
1 TABLESPOON CHOPPED SCALLIONS
1 TEASPOON SESAME OIL
3 TABLESPOONS VEGETABLE OIL
⅔ CUP BEAN SPROUTS
4 OUNCES (1 CUP) FRESH SHIITAKE
   MUSHROOMS, SLICED
¾ CUP DICED CHINESE BARBECUED PORK
1½ TABLESPOONS HOISIN OR OYSTER SAUCE
1 HEAPING TEASPOON CHINESE CHILI
   GARLIC SAUCE

In a medium bowl, beat together the eggs, soy sauce, coriander, scallions, and sesame oil. Set aside.

Heat the vegetable oil in a wok over medium-high heat. Sauté the bean sprouts and mushrooms until cooked through, about 3 minutes. Add the pork and warm through, about 1 more minute. Drizzle with the hoisin sauce and chili garlic sauce, and toss thoroughly to combine.

Lower the heat to medium. Pour the beaten egg mixture over the meat and vegetables, and cook, stirring occasionally, until large curds form, about 2 to 3 minutes. Once the eggs are cooked to your liking, remove them from the heat. Cut the scramble into wedges and serve with toast.

CHICKEN SAUSAGE AND GOAT CHEESE SCRAMBLE

In the mood for a casual, diner-style breakfast, but unwilling to brave the sleepy morning crowds to get it? This scramble will be ready on the stovetop in just about fifteen minutes, leaving you plenty of time to sleep in. Serve it with hearty slices of buttered toast or hash browns—or both!

SERVES 2 TO 4

2 TABLESPOONS VEGETABLE OIL

¾ POUND CHICKEN SAUSAGE,
  CASINGS REMOVED

½ MEDIUM SWEET ONION, MINCED

6 EGGS, BEATEN

4 OUNCES GOAT CHEESE

1 PLUM TOMATO, DICED

1 TABLESPOON FLAT-LEAF PARSLEY,
  FINELY CHOPPED

KOSHER SALT AND FRESHLY GROUND
  BLACK PEPPER

HOT SAUCE (OPTIONAL)

Heat the oil n a wok over medium-high heat. Add the sausage and crumble it with a spatula as it browns and cooks through, about 6 to 7 minutes. Add the onions and cook until softened, about 5 minutes.

Reduce the heat to medium. Pour in the eggs and cook until they just begin to firm up, 1 to 2 minutes. Stir in the goat cheese, tomato, and parsley, and season to taste with salt and pepper. Continue cooking the eggs to your liking.

Dish up the scramble, and drizzle with hot sauce.

THE ULTIMATE FRIED EGG SANDWICH

Whether for a hearty lunch or casual supper, few things approach perfection as closely as a delicious fried egg sandwich. My secret to this indulgent version is to use an extra yolk (you can easily save the remaining eggwhite for another use—to add to tomorrow's omelet, for example, or to glaze a pie). Piled with peppery arugula, thick slices of summer-sweet tomato, and melting slices of Taleggio cheese, this simple sandwich will rescue you on those harried days when you just need something quick, satisfying, and delicious to tide you over.

MAKES 1 SANDWICH

1 EGG, PLUS 1 YOLK
1 TABLESPOON UNSALTED BUTTER
2 SLICES SOURDOUGH BREAD
2 OUNCES TALEGGIO CHEESE,
   THINLY SLICED
1 TABLESPOON OLIVE OIL
KOSHER SALT AND FRESHLY GROUND
   BLACK PEPPER
1 SMALL HANDFUL ARUGULA
2 SLICES RIPE TOMATO (PREFERABLY HEIRLOOM)

Crack the egg into a small bowl and carefully add the extra yolk.

Heat the wok over medium heat. Lightly butter one side of each of the bread slices. Pile one unbuttered side with the Taleggio and toast both slices buttered side down in the wok until golden brown. Set aside.

Still over medium heat, heat the oil and fry the egg and extra yolk to your liking. For a firm egg white but a runny yolk, cover the wok and check periodically—it should take about 3 minutes for the white to cook through and become opaque. Season lightly with salt and pepper.

Place the egg on the melted cheese. Top with the arugula, the tomato slices, and the other slice of bread, and enjoy!

CHORIZO, HARISSA, AND POTATO HASH

Harissa, a chili sauce widely used in North Africa and Morocco, is a wonderfully flavorful condiment that lends an exotic flavor to an everyday sausage-and-potato hash. If your local grocery store doesn't carry this ingredient, look for it online; it's widely available. This hash is the ideal accompaniment for fried or scrambled eggs, hot coffee, and the Sunday paper.

SERVES 4

4 TABLESPOONS OLIVE OIL, DIVIDED
1½ TEASPOONS HARISSA PASTE
¾ POUND FINGERLING POTATOES, QUARTERED
KOSHER SALT AND FRESHLY GROUND
  BLACK PEPPER
1 MEDIUM SWEET ONION, FINELY DICED
½ GREEN BELL PEPPER, DICED
1½ POUNDS FRESH CHORIZO SAUSAGE,
  CASINGS REMOVED
CHOPPED FRESH PARSLEY, FOR GARNISH

TO SERVE:
FRIED OR SCRAMBLED EGGS

Preheat the oven to 400 degrees F.

In a small bowl, whisk together 2 tablespoons of the oil and the harissa paste.

Toss the potatoes with the oil and harissa, and season lightly with salt and pepper. Arrange the potatoes in a single layer on a baking sheet. Bake until cooked through and golden, about 25 minutes, stirring and turning the potatoes midway through cooking to ensure even browning. Set the cooked potatoes aside.

Meanwhile, in a wok, heat the remaining 2 tablespoons of oil over high heat. Add the onions and peppers and cook until softened, about 6 to 7 minutes. Add the chorizo to the wok and cook through, about 4 to 5 minutes. Add the roasted harissa potatoes and toss to combine. Taste and add salt and pepper if necessary. Sprinkle with the parsley.

Serve the hash with fried or scrambled eggs.

BRIE AND CHIVE OMELET

Perfect for breakfast with a side of roasted potatoes or alongside a simple salad for a light supper, this omelet is elegant in its simplicity and big on flavor. For a nice twist, try substituting two duck eggs for the chicken eggs.

SERVES 1

1 TABLESPOON UNSALTED BUTTER
3 EGGS, OR 2 DUCK EGGS, BEATEN
1 TABLESPOON FRESH CHIVES,
   FINELY CHOPPED
1 TEASPOON MINCED FRESH CHERVIL
KOSHER SALT AND FRESHLY GROUND
   BLACK PEPPER
2 OUNCES BRIE, SLICED, RIND
   DISCARDED IF PREFERRED

TO SERVE:
ROASTED POTATOES OR TOAST

Heat the butter in a wok over medium heat. Pour the eggs into the wok, and stir gently for 1 minute to create large curds.

Sprinkle the chives and chervil over the eggs and lightly season with salt and pepper. Lay the slices of Brie on ½ of the eggs. Continue cooking the omelet until the eggs are just set, about 2 minutes. Gently fold the omelet over the Brie-covered half to encase the cheese.

Slide the omelet onto a plate and serve with roasted potatoes or toast.

MAINS

BEEF + PORK
CHICKEN
SEAFOOD
VEGETARIAN

BEEF + PORK

RECIPES

CHICKEN-FRIED STEAK WITH COUNTRY PAN GRAVY

Served over mashed potatoes and blanketed in a thick, creamy thyme-flecked onion gravy, these chicken-fried steaks epitomize real comfort food. If you have any leftover gravy, try it over hot breakfast biscuits the next morning.

SERVES 4

FOR THE CHICKEN-FRIED STEAKS:
FOUR 6- TO 7-OUNCE TENDERIZED BEEF CUBE STEAKS
2 TEASPOONS KOSHER SALT
2 TEASPOONS GARLIC POWDER
¾ TEASPOON FRESHLY GROUND BLACK PEPPER
1 CUP BUTTERMILK
2 EGGS
1 TABLESPOON HOT SAUCE
2 CUPS ALL-PURPOSE FLOUR
¼ CUP VEGETABLE OIL

FOR THE GRAVY:
2 TABLESPOONS UNSALTED BUTTER
   OR BACON DRIPPINGS
1 MEDIUM SWEET ONION, THINLY SLICED
¼ CUP ALL-PURPOSE FLOUR
1 CUP CHICKEN STOCK
1¾ CUPS HALF-AND-HALF
¼ TO ½ TEASPOON RED PEPPER FLAKES
¾ TEASPOON DRIED THYME
KOSHER SALT AND FRESHLY GROUND
   BLACK PEPPER

TO SERVE:
MASHED POTATOES

To make the steaks, pound them to ¼-inch thickness and season both sides with the salt, garlic powder, and pepper.

In a shallow dish, beat together the buttermilk, eggs, and hot sauce. Put the flour in another shallow dish or on a plate.

Dredge the steaks in the flour, then in the buttermilk mixture (letting the excess drip off), then again in the flour, and place on a tray or baking sheet. Let the steaks rest for 15 minutes so that the breading starts to dry and adheres better.

Heat the oil in a wok over medium-high heat. Fry the steaks 2 at a time in the oil until golden brown, 3 to 4 minutes per side. Repeat with the remaining steaks.

To make the gravy, lower the heat to medium and add the butter to the remaining bit of oil and drippings in the wok. Fry the onions until golden, about 7 minutes. Add the flour and cook for 1 minute. Add the stock and half-and-half and cook, stirring, until the gravy bubbles and thickens. Stir in the red pepper flakes to taste and thyme. Season to taste with salt and pepper.

To serve, place each steak on a plate atop mashed potatoes and pour pan gravy over it.

RED SAUCE SPAGHETTI WITH BISON MEATBALLS

Meatballs are traditionally made with three types of meat—beef, pork, or veal—but these leaner, less fussy bison meatballs are so flavorful, they just might become your new favorite. The quality of the red sauce depends largely on the olive oil and tomatoes you use, so get the best you can find. (Canned San Marzano tomatoes are particularly wonderful in this recipe.)

SERVES 4

FOR THE MEATBALLS:
1 POUND GROUND BISON
¾ CUP PARMESAN OR ROMANO CHEESE, FINELY GRATED, PLUS MORE FOR GARNISH
¼ CUP FLAT-LEAF PARSLEY, FINELY CHOPPED
1 TEASPOON KOSHER SALT
½ TEASPOON FRESHLY GROUND BLACK PEPPER
1 EGG
2 CLOVES GARLIC, FINELY CHOPPED
¾ CUP BREAD CRUMBS
⅓ CUP MILK
½ CUP EXTRA-VIRGIN OLIVE OIL
1 LARGE SWEET ONION, FINELY DICED

FOR THE RED SAUCE SPAGHETTI:
ONE 28-OUNCE CAN WHOLE SAN MARZANO TOMATOES OR OTHER TOP-QUALITY PLUM TOMATOES
ONE 6-OUNCE CAN TOMATO PASTE
¼ CUP DRY WHITE WINE
4 CLOVES GARLIC, FINELY MINCED
2 TEASPOONS CHOPPED FRESH OREGANO, OR 1 TEASPOON DRIED
¾ CUP CHOPPED FRESH BASIL
PINCH OF RED PEPPER FLAKES
KOSHER SALT AND FRESHLY GROUND BLACK PEPPER
12 OUNCES UNCOOKED SPAGHETTI

To make the meatballs, in a large bowl, combine the bison, Parmesan, parsley, salt, and pepper. Mix in the egg, garlic, bread crumbs, and milk. Take care not to overwork the mixture or the meatballs will be dense and tough. Gently shape into balls about 1½ inches in diameter.

Heat the oil in a wok over medium-high heat.
Sauté the onion until golden, about 5 minutes.
Add the meatballs and fry in batches until lightly
browned on all sides.

To make the red spaghetti sauce, when all the
meatballs are browned, return them to the wok.
Add the tomatoes, tomato paste, wine, garlic,
oregano, basil, and red pepper flakes, and season
lightly with salt and pepper. Partially cover the
wok and lower the heat to medium. Simmer the
sauce and meatballs for 25 to 30 minutes.

Meanwhile, bring a pot of salted water to a boil.
Cook the spaghetti according to the package
directions and drain.

Serve the spaghetti topped with generous
ladlefuls of sauce and meatballs, and garnish
with Parmesan.

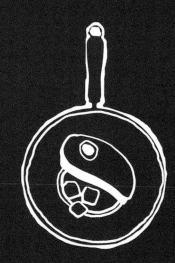

EASY, SPICY BEEF AND BROCCOLI STIR-FRY

Growing up in a Cantonese household, I've always loved eating my mom's beef and broccoli. When I married my spice-loving Hunanese husband, I started cooking this dish for him, only to find him doctoring his portion with Asian chili sauce every time it made an appearance at dinner. One night I decided to sneak some chili sauce directly into the marinade for the meat. And you know what? That's the version we both love the best!

SERVES 2

¾ POUND HANGAR OR SKIRT STEAK,
   CUT AGAINST THE GRAIN INTO
   ¼-INCH-THICK PIECES
1½ TEASPOONS LIGHT SOY SAUCE
1 TEASPOON DARK SOY SAUCE
2 HEAPING TABLESPOONS OYSTER OR
   CHEE HOU SAUCE
1 TABLESPOON SHAO-HSING WINE OR DRY SHERRY
1 HEAPING TABLESPOON ASIAN CHILI SAUCE
   (SUCH AS SAMBAL OELEK)
½ TEASPOON SUGAR
¼ TEASPOON FRESHLY GROUND BLACK PEPPER
1 TABLESPOON CORNSTARCH
2 CLOVES GARLIC, FINELY MINCED
3 TABLESPOONS VEGETABLE OIL, DIVIDED
1 LARGE HEAD BROCCOLI, FLORETS ONLY
KOSHER SALT

TO SERVE:
STEAMED RICE

In a large bowl, combine the steak with the light and dark soy sauces, oyster sauce, wine, chili sauce, sugar, pepper, and cornstarch. Let marinate for 15 minutes.

Meanwhile, combine the garlic and 2 tablespoons of the oil in a cold wok. This initial cold infusion in the oil will maximize the flavor of the garlic without its burning. Bring the heat up to high while keeping a close eye on the garlic. As soon as the garlic begins to turn golden, add the broccoli. Cook the broccoli until crisp-tender, about 4 to 5 minutes. Stir only occasionally to allow the broccoli plenty of contact time with the wok, so it develops a bit of a sear. (If you prefer your broccoli very soft, add 1 or 2 tablespoons of water to the wok and cover for another 1 to

2 minutes.) Once the broccoli is cooked to your liking, remove it from the wok and set aside.

Heat the remaining tablespoon of oil in the wok over high heat. Add the meat and sear it, moving it only occasionally with a spatula to allow it plenty of contact time with the wok. Cook the meat to your liking—about 3 minutes for medium doneness. Add the broccoli and 2 or 3 tablespoons of water and toss everything to combine. (The water bubbles up, then reduces with the pan drippings and makes a nice sauce.) Taste and season lightly with salt if needed. As soon as the sauce bubbles up and thickens, serve the beef and broccoli over steamed rice.

MY MOTHER-IN-LAW'S STIR-FRIED CABBAGE AND BACON

When my mother-in-law's husband unexpectedly passed away back in the '70s, she found herself a young widow struggling to balance the tasks of raising two young kids and maintaining a full-time job. Still, she found the time to prepare quick and delicious, home-cooked meals each night—an admirable feat! This recipe was a favorite of my husband's while growing up. To this day, it's our go-to dish when we have less than fifteen minutes to throw together a weeknight meal. With steamed rice and fried eggs, it makes a great quick-and-easy supper.

SERVES 2

5 SLICES BACON, CUT ROUGHLY INTO
   1-INCH SQUARES
½ MEDIUM HEAD CABBAGE, CUT
   ROUGHLY INTO 1-INCH SQUARES
PINCH OF RED PEPPER FLAKES
2 TEASPOONS LIGHT SOY SAUCE

TO SERVE:
SESAME OIL, STEAMED RICE, FRIED
   EGGS (OPTIONAL)

In a wok over high heat, fry the bacon until crisp, 3 to 4 minutes.

Add the cabbage to the wok and cook in the rendered bacon fat until the cabbage is tender but still slightly crisp, about 4 minutes. Stir only occasionally, so the cabbage has enough contact time in the wok to sear. The edges of the cabbage leaves will turn golden brown.

Add the red pepper flakes and drizzle in the soy sauce. Toss thoroughly and serve alone or with more soy sauce and a drizzle of sesame oil over steamed rice and fried eggs.

WOK-SEARED RIBEYES WITH EASY HERB BUTTER

For a special night in, try this easy but impressive meal: succulent steaks with your favorite traditional steak house sides, like mashed potatoes and Holiday Creamed Spinach with Parmesan (page 112). Herb butter may sound fancy, but it's easy to make and keeps wonderfully if tightly wrapped in the fridge. Leftover herb butter is perfect to toss into hot pasta or slather over hot dinner rolls. Note: Allow an hour before you begin cooking for the steaks to rest at room temperature; they will cook more evenly.

SERVES 2 TO 4

FOR THE HERB BUTTER:

½ CUP (1 STICK) UNSALTED BUTTER, SOFTENED
1 TABLESPOON FRESH CHIVES, FINELY CHOPPED
1 TEASPOON CHOPPED FRESH THYME
2 TABLESPOONS GRATED PARMESAN

FOR THE STEAKS:

2 TABLESPOONS VEGETABLE OIL
3 CLOVES GARLIC, CRUSHED BUT STILL WHOLE
TWO 1½-INCH-THICK RIBEYE STEAKS,
  ABOUT 1 POUND EACH
KOSHER SALT AND FRESHLY GROUND
  BLACK PEPPER

An hour before you plan to cook the steaks, remove them from the refrigerator and let them come to room temperature.

To make the herb butter, in a small bowl, combine the butter, chives, thyme, and Parmesan. Roll up the butter in plastic wrap and shape it lightly into a cylinder with your hands. Refrigerate the butter to firm up, at least 30 minutes.

To make the steaks, heat the oil and garlic in a wok over high heat. Allow the garlic to brown (but be careful not to let it burn) and infuse the oil for 2 minutes, then discard it.

Season the steaks with salt and pepper. Cook the steaks in the garlic–infused oil for about 5 minutes per side for medium-rare. Do not move them around too much; allow them plenty of contact time with the wok to develop a nice sear.

Transfer the steaks to plates and top with 1 or 2 tablespoons of the herb butter. Serve as soon as the butter has melted.

EASY TAILGATE CHILI

Despite a lengthy ingredient list, this chili is one of the easiest meals you'll ever put together. Packed with ground beef and Italian sausage—and fragrant with a heady mix of spices—this crowd-pleaser will have people clamoring for thirds. Serve it at your next game night, with plenty of tortilla chips, sour cream, guacamole, and cheese on hand so your guests can customize their portions. You can make it up to two days ahead; store it covered in the refrigerator.

SERVES 6 TO 8

3 TABLESPOONS VEGETABLE OIL, DIVIDED

1 LARGE SWEET ONION, FINELY CHOPPED

4 CLOVES GARLIC, FINELY CHOPPED

1½ POUNDS GROUND BEEF

KOSHER SALT AND FRESHLY GROUND BLACK PEPPER

1½ POUNDS MILD ITALIAN SAUSAGE,
   CASINGS REMOVED

3 JALAPEÑOS, SEEDED AND CHOPPED

1 LARGE RED BELL PEPPER, SEEDED AND CHOPPED

ONE 28-OUNCE CAN CRUSHED TOMATOES

ONE 6-OUNCE CAN TOMATO PASTE

ONE 12-OUNCE BOTTLE LAGER-STYLE BEER

3 TEASPOONS GROUND CUMIN

¼ CUP CHILI POWDER

2 TABLESPOONS SWEET PAPRIKA

1 TABLESPOON DRIED OREGANO

2 TABLESPOONS TABASCO SAUCE

2 TABLESPOONS WORCESTERSHIRE SAUCE

1 TABLESPOON BROWN SUGAR

TO SERVE:

TORTILLA CHIPS, SOUR CREAM, GUACAMOLE,
   GRATED CHEESE, AND CHOPPED RED ONION

Heat 1 tablespoon of the oil in a wok over medium-high heat and sauté the onion until golden, 3 to 5 minutes. Add the garlic and cook for another minute. Transfer the mixture to a bowl.

Season the ground beef to taste with salt and pepper. Heat the remaining 2 tablespoons of oil in the wok and brown the beef, stirring for about 5 minutes. Transfer the beef to a bowl.

Brown the sausage in the wok for about 5 minutes. Return the onion mixture and the beef to the wok, then add the jalapeños, bell pepper, crushed tomatoes, tomato paste, beer, cumin, chili powder, paprika, oregano, Tabasco, Worcestershire, and brown sugar. Cover the wok and simmer over medium-low heat for 2 hours, stirring it until every 30 minutes or so.

MAINS   59

BIG BOY PULLED-PORK SANDWICHES

As much as I love tending my smoker for ten-plus hours to perfect a juicy smoked pork butt, this low-maintenance, quick-cooking (by comparison) stovetop pulled pork is almost as good as the real deal. Just add all the ingredients to your wok, give the pork a stir every thirty minutes or so, and in three and a half hours you'll have a nice, saucy batch of succulent pork to pile high on hamburger buns. Best of all, it's a snap to put together—the ideal make-ahead dish for a crowd! Covered and refrigerated, it will keep nicely for up to two days before serving.

SERVES 8

3 POUNDS BONELESS PORK SHOULDER,
    CUT INTO 4 EQUAL PIECES
ONE 6-OUNCE CAN TOMATO PASTE
½ CUP APPLE CIDER VINEGAR
3 TABLESPOONS WORCESTERSHIRE SAUCE
¼ CUP DARK BROWN SUGAR, PACKED
¼ CUP DIJON MUSTARD
1 TEASPOON ONION POWDER
1 TEASPOON GARLIC POWDER
1½ TEASPOONS KOSHER SALT
¾ TEASPOON FRESHLY GROUND BLACK PEPPER
2 TABLESPOONS SWEET PAPRIKA

1 TABLESPOON GROUND CUMIN
3 TEASPOONS CHILI POWDER
¾ CUP CHICKEN STOCK
2 TABLESPOONS LIQUID SMOKE

TO SERVE:
HAMBURGER BUNS
YOUR FAVORITE COLESLAW

Combine all the ingredients except the liquid
smoke in a wok over medium-low heat. Partially
cover the wok and simmer for 3 hours, stirring
the pork every half hour or so, to ensure even
cooking. When the pork is completely tender
and shreds easily with a fork, remove the
wok from the heat.

Remove the pork from the sauce and place it on
a platter. Shred the pork with 2 forks, then return
all the meat and juices back to the sauce in the
wok. Continue simmering, uncovered, stirring
occasionally, until the sauce reduces
a bit, about 30 minutes. Stir in the liquid
smoke just before serving.

Serve the pork on the buns and pile them high
with coleslaw.

RED-BRAISED PORK BELLY OVER JASMINE RICE

Red cooking is a Shanghainese technique that involves braising meat, tofu, or eggs in a richly flavored dark soy sauce. When I was a young girl, my parents used to take me to a Shanghainese restaurant every weekend for its famous red-cooked pork belly, which came in a traditional clay pot on a bed of jade-colored bok choy vegetables. Years later, my husband and I make this dish at least once a week in the fall and winter. The texture of the pork belly after it has been braised for three hours is magnificent—each bite yields a morsel of lacquered pork rind, then a soft striation of fat, and finally a nugget of tender meat. This is a classic wok recipe.

SERVES 8 AS A SIDE DISH

3 POUNDS PORK BELLY,
   CUT INTO 2-INCH CUBES
ONE 3-INCH-PIECE FRESH GINGER,
   SLICED INTO 4 PIECES
4 SCALLIONS, CUT INTO 3-INCH PIECES
1/3 CUP DARK BROWN SUGAR, PACKED
1/2 CUP SHAO-HSING WINE OR DRY SHERRY
1/2 CUP DARK SOY SAUCE
1/2 CUP LIGHT SOY SAUCE
4 CUPS CHICKEN STOCK (PREFERABLY HOMEMADE)
4 STAR ANISE
2 STICKS CINNAMON
1/3 CUP HOISIN SAUCE

TO SERVE:
STEAMED RICE AND STIR-FRIED VEGETABLES

Slice the pork belly into 1-inch-thick strips, then slice into chunks about 1-inch-thick and 3-inches long.

In a wok over medium-high heat, combine the ginger, scallions, brown sugar, wine, both soy sauces, stock, star anise, and cinnamon. Add the pork to the liquid. If the pork is not covered with the liquid, add enough water to just cover. Bring to a boil, then lower the heat to medium-low to maintain a simmer.

Cook the pork, stirring occasionally, until the pork is tender when pierced with a knife, about 3 hours.

Strain the ginger, scallions, star anise, and cinnamon out of the braising liquid and discard. With a ladle, skim off the clear fat that's collected at the surface of the braising liquid, and discard.

Remove the pork from the braising liquid and set aside. Add the hoisin sauce to the braising liquid, and simmer for about 15 to 20 minutes, until slightly thickened. Add the pork back into the sauce, and heat thoroughly.

Serve the pork and sauce over steamed rice.

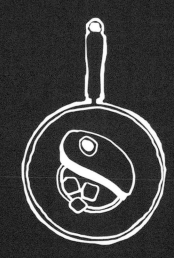

CARNITAS

Because authentic *carnitas* are often cooked in plenty of lard, many modern recipes call for a simmer in water or stock in a bid to cut down on the fat. This recipe is a nice compromise: the addition of a little lard or vegetable oil to the cooking process keeps the meat extra moist, while garlic, onions, bay leaves, orange juice, and cumin give it plenty of flavor without any fat. A final crisping under the broiler ensures plenty of lovely crunchy pork bits to pile into warm tortillas.

SERVES 6

2½ POUNDS BONELESS PORK SHOULDER,
   CUT INTO 2-INCH CHUNKS
2 TABLESPOONS KOSHER SALT
5 GARLIC CLOVES
1 MEDIUM YELLOW ONION, QUARTERED
3 BAY LEAVES
JUICE OF ONE ORANGE
1 TEASPOON GROUND CUMIN
⅓ CUP LARD OR VEGETABLE OIL
1½ CUP WATER

TO SERVE:
WARM TORTILLAS, LIME WEDGES, GUACAMOLE,
   SALSA, CHOPPED ONION, AND CILANTRO

Combine all ingredients in a wok. Cover and cook over medium heat until tender, about 3 to 3½ hours. Stir occasionally, making sure all of the pork spends some time submerged in the liquid and lard. (If necessary, add another ½ cup of water to the wok midway through the cooking process if the meat begins to look dry.)

Remove and discard the bay leaves. Transfer the pork to a large casserole dish and spoon a few tablespoons of the cooking liquid over it. Shred the pork using 2 forks.

Preheat the broiler.

Broil the pork until the surface crisps, about 5 minutes. Remove the pan from the oven and fluff up the pork with a fork, mixing the crisped layer into the moist meat underneath. Broil it one more time until the surface crisps, about 5 more minutes. (Keep a close eye on the pork to ensure it doesn't burn.)

Serve the *carnitas* with warm tortillas, lime wedges, guacamole, salsa, onion, and cilantro.

SWEET-AND-SOUR PORK

Ambivalent about the too-sweet, gloppy takeout version of sweet-and-sour pork? The best part about cooking this popular recipe at home is that you can adjust the amount of sugar and use fresher ingredients. Tender, marinated pork is first dredged in flour, then fried and tossed in the classic sauce made with Chinese red vinegar, pineapple juice, and fresh vegetables.

SERVES 4

FOR THE PORK:
1 POUND PORK TENDERLOIN,
   CUT INTO BITE-SIZE PIECES
1 TABLESPOON LIGHT SOY SAUCE
1 TEASPOON DARK SOY SAUCE
1 TABLESPOON SHAO-HSING WINE
   OR DRY SHERRY
1 TEASPOON SESAME OIL

FOR THE SAUCE:
2 TABLESPOONS VEGETABLE OIL
½ MEDIUM SWEET ONION,
   SLICED INTO ¾-INCH PIECES
½ RED BELL PEPPER, SLICED INTO ¾-INCH PIECES
½ GREEN BELL PEPPER, SLICED INTO
   ¾-INCH PIECES
2 CLOVES GARLIC, CHOPPED
3 TABLESPOONS KETCHUP
3 TABLESPOONS SUGAR

1 CUP PINEAPPLE CHUNKS
⅓ CUP PINEAPPLE JUICE
¼ CUP CHINESE RED VINEGAR
1 TABLESPOON CORNSTARCH DISSOLVED IN
   2 TABLESPOONS WATER

FOR THE COATING:
¼ CUP ALL-PURPOSE FLOUR
¼ CUP CORNSTARCH

VEGETABLE OR PEANUT OIL FOR FRYING

TO SERVE:
STEAMED RICE

In a large bowl, combine the pork, light and dark soy sauces, wine, and sesame oil. Let the pork marinate for 30 minutes.

Meanwhile, make the sauce. In a saucepan, heat the oil over high heat. Add the onion and red and green peppers and stir-fry until cooked through, 6 to 7 minutes. Lower the heat to medium. Add the garlic, ketchup, sugar, pineapple chunks, juice, and vinegar. Cook, stirring, until the sauce reduces slightly, 4 to 6 minutes. Pour in the dissolved cornstarch and stir until the sauce bubbles up. Take the sauce off the heat and set aside.

To make the coating, combine the flour and cornstarch in a medium bowl. Dredge the pork in the mixture until well coated. Shake off the excess.

In a wok, heat several inches of oil to 350 degrees F, measuring with a deep-fry thermometer. Fry the pork in small batches until golden, about 3 minutes per batch. Set the cooked pork aside on paper towels to drain.

Once you have fried all the pork, discard the oil in the wok. Lower the heat to medium and return the pork to the wok. Pour the sauce over the pork and toss to coat. Serve over steamed rice.

ITALIAN SAUSAGE AND PEPPERS OVER CREAMY POLENTA

One of my favorite comfort foods—cheesy grits—is made even better with wok-seared sausages and a soft tangle of peppers and onions. This is a meal that's welcome whether for breakfast, lunch, or dinner.

SERVES 2 TO 4

1½ CUPS WHOLE MILK

1¾ CUPS WATER

¾ CUP POLENTA

3 TABLESPOONS BUTTER

1¼ CUPS GRATED PARMESAN
   OR PECORINO CHEESE

KOSHER SALT AND FRESHLY GROUND
   BLACK PEPPER

3 TABLESPOONS OLIVE OIL, DIVIDED

1½ POUNDS ITALIAN SAUSAGE

½ RED BELL PEPPER,
   THINLY SLICED

½ YELLOW BELL PEPPER,
   THINLY SLICED

½ GREEN BELL PEPPER,
   THINLY SLICED

½ MEDIUM SWEET ONION,
   THINLY SLICED

½ TEASPOON DRIED OREGANO OR MARJORAM

RED PEPPER FLAKES

In a large saucepan over high heat, combine the milk and water and bring to a boil. Lower the heat to medium and add the polenta. Stir in the butter and continue cooking, stirring occasionally, until the polenta is cooked through, bubbles up and thickens, about 20 minutes. Stir in the cheese, season to taste with salt and pepper, and keep warm.

Meanwhile, heat 2 tablespoons of the oil in a wok over medium-high heat. Fry the sausages until nicely browned on all sides and cooked through, 7 to 8 minutes. Remove the sausages from the wok and set aside. Add the remaining tablespoon of oil and the peppers and onions to the drippings in the wok. Cook over high heat until the onions are golden brown and the peppers are slightly blistered, 6 to 7 minutes. Season with the oregano, a pinch or two of red pepper flakes, and salt to taste.

Return the sausages to the wok and toss to combine. Divide the polenta among the plates and top each portion with some of the sausage mixture.

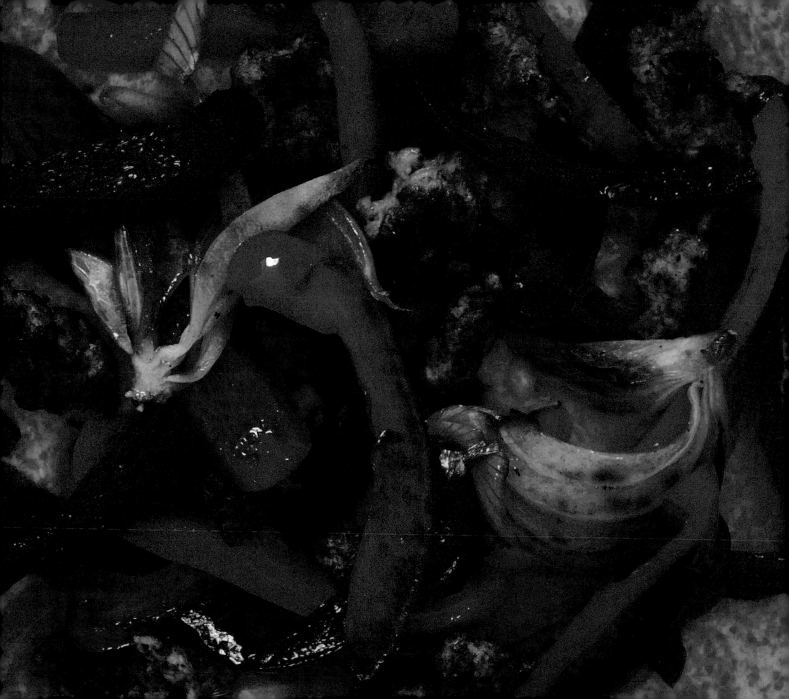

MOM'S STICKY RICE WITH CHINESE SAUSAGE, MUSHROOMS, AND SHRIMP

When I was growing up, not one birthday or holiday passed without my mom's signature sticky rice on the table. This flavorful rice, packed with Chinese sausage, mushrooms, and dried shrimp, was one of my favorite side dishes; it also appeared in lieu of traditional stuffing on Thanksgiving and Christmas. I hope this special recipe finds a place in your repertoire, as it has in mine.

SERVES 6

8 OUNCES (2 CUPS) DRIED SHIITAKE MUSHROOMS

½ CUP CHINESE DRIED SHRIMP

2 TABLESPOONS SHAO-HSING WINE OR DRY SHERRY

2½ CUPS CHINESE OR JAPANESE SHORT-GRAIN ("STICKY") RICE

3 CUPS LOW-SODIUM CHICKEN BROTH, DIVIDED

6 TABLESPOONS VEGETABLE OIL, DIVIDED

2 TABLESPOONS LIGHT SOY SAUCE, DIVIDED

⅔ CUP SCALLIONS, FINELY CHOPPED

7 CHINESE SAUSAGES (ABOUT 8 TO 9 OUNCES), THINLY SLICED

½ CUP CILANTRO, FINELY CHOPPED

2 TO 3 TABLESPOONS OYSTER SAUCE

Soak the dried mushrooms in warm water until softened, about 2 hours. Rinse the dried shrimps and toss them in the wine (this eliminates their "fishy" flavor).

When the mushrooms are hydrated and softened, slice them thinly and set aside.

Wash the rice in warm water and drain. Repeat until the water runs clear. Steam the rice in 2¾ cups of the broth in a rice cooker or a covered saucepan on the stovetop over medium heat until cooked through and tender, about 30 minutes. (If using a saucepan, watch the rice so that the bottom doesn't scorch, lowering the heat to medium-low if necessary.)

Heat 2 tablespoons of the oil in a wok over high heat. Add the shrimp and the remaining ¼ cup of broth to the wok and cook until the broth is absorbed, 3 to 4 minutes. Remove the shrimp and set aside.

Heat 2 more tablespoons of the oil in the wok over high heat. Cook the mushrooms for 3 to 4 minutes, stirring only occasionally so they develop a seared surface. Season with 1 tablespoon of the soy sauce and add the scallions. Continue cooking for another minute, then remove the mushroom mixture and set aside.

Heat the remaining 2 tablespoons of oil in the wok over medium heat. Fry the sausages in the oil until cooked through, about 3 minutes. Stir in the mushroom mixture and the shrimp. Add the cooked rice and the cilantro and toss thoroughly to combine. Season with the remaining tablespoon of soy sauce and oyster sauce to taste, toss again, and serve.

WINTRY BEEF STEW

A long-simmering beef stew is ideally suited for a wok, because you can brown the meat and braise it all in the same vessel. This recipe is accented with fresh herbs, smoky bacon, and root vegetables that lend a lovely natural sweetness. Serve this stew with thick pieces of hearty whole grain bread, over buttered noodles, or with rice.

SERVES 6

3 POUNDS STEWING BEEF (SUCH AS CHUCK
  SHOULDER ROAST), CUT INTO 1-INCH PIECES
¼ CUP ALL-PURPOSE FLOUR
1 TABLESPOON KOSHER SALT
1 TEASPOON FRESHLY GROUND BLACK PEPPER
3 TABLESPOONS VEGETABLE OIL
4 SLICES THICK-CUT BACON
1 LARGE SWEET ONION, DICED
4 CLOVES GARLIC
2 SPRIGS FRESH ROSEMARY
4 SPRIGS FRESH THYME
2 BAY LEAVES
1½ CUPS DRY RED WINE
3 CUPS BEEF BROTH
¼ CUP TOMATO PASTE
1½ TABLESPOONS BROWN SUGAR
2 TABLESPOONS WORCESTERSHIRE SAUCE
2 MEDIUM CARROTS, PEELED AND
  CUT INTO ½-INCH PIECES

2 LARGE PARSNIPS, PEELED AND
  CUT INTO ½-INCH PIECES
2 STALKS CELERY, CUT INTO ½-INCH PIECES
4 MEDIUM YUKON GOLD OR
  RED POTATOES, QUARTERED
1 CUP FROZEN PEAS

TO SERVE:
RICE, NOODLES, OR TOASTED BREAD

Pat the beef dry. In a large, shallow dish, toss the beef with the flour, salt, and pepper.

Heat the oil in a wok over high heat. Divide the beef into 3 batches and brown each batch on all sides until it develops a nice golden brown crust. Set aside.

Cook the bacon in the wok over medium-high heat until crisp, about 5 minutes. Add the onions and cook in the bacon fat until golden brown, about 5 minutes. Return the beef to the wok along with the garlic, rosemary, thyme, bay leaves, wine, broth, tomato paste, brown sugar, and Worcestershire. Bring the liquid to a boil, then lower the heat to medium-low. Partially cover the wok and let the stew simmer until almost fork-tender, about 2 hours, stirring occasionally.

Add the carrots, parsnips, celery, and potatoes to the stew. Simmer, partially covered, until the vegetables are completely tender, about 1 hour. Stir in the frozen peas and simmer for another 5 minutes to warm them through. Discard the garlic cloves, bay leaves, and herb sprigs. Taste and adjust the seasoning.

Serve the stew in big bowls over rice or noodles, or with a thick slice of toasted bread.

HENRY'S GINGERY PORK POT STICKERS

One of my favorite ways to spend an afternoon with my husband is sitting at the kitchen table, rolling out pot sticker dough and filling each one with gingery pork filling. We often make a large batch to freeze for quick meals later on in the week. My husband is an expert at frying pot stickers—soft and steamed through on top, with a crunchy, golden brown bottom. His technique is now preserved in this recipe! It works best in a well-seasoned, flat-bottomed wok or a large nonstick pan.

MAKES ABOUT 30 POT STICKERS

FOR THE FILLING:
1 POUND REGULAR (NOT LEAN) GROUND PORK
3 TABLESPOONS GINGER, FINELY MINCED
8 CLOVES GARLIC, FINELY MINCED
4½ CUPS LOOSELY PACKED, FINELY
  SHREDDED NAPA CABBAGE
2 TABLESPOON LIGHT SOY SAUCE
2 TABLESPOON DARK SOY SAUCE
2 TABLESPOON SHAO-HSING WINE OR DRY SHERRY
2 TABLESPOON SESAME OIL
½ TEASPOON KOSHER SALT

FOR THE DOUGH:
4 CUPS ALL-PURPOSE FLOUR
½ TEASPOON KOSHER SALT
1½ CUPS HOT WATER

¼ CUP VEGETABLE OIL, PLUS MORE FOR OILING
  THE DOUGH

FOR THE DIPPING SAUCE:
1 TABLESPOON GINGER, FINELY SLIVERED
2 TABLESPOONS CHINESE BLACK
  OR RICE VINEGAR
2 TABLESPOONS LIGHT SOY SAUCE
1 TABLESPOON ASIAN CHILI SAUCE
  (SUCH AS SAMBAL OELEK)
2 TEASPOONS SESAME OIL
PINCH OF SUGAR (OPTIONAL)

To make the filling, in a large bowl, stir together all the ingredients until just combined. (Do not overmix, or your filling will be dense.) Cover the filling and refrigerator it while you make the dough.

To make the dough, in a separate large bowl, combine the flour, salt, and water. Turn out the dough onto a board and knead for about 5 minutes, until it starts to come together—if at any point the dough feels too dry, make an indent on top, add another couple of tablespoons of hot water, and work it in. If the dough feels too wet and sticky, add another 1 to 2 tablespoons of flour. After kneading, the dough should be soft and smooth.

Place the dough back in the bowl and lightly oil the surface. Cover with plastic wrap and let rest for 30 minutes at room temperature. Do not refrigerate, or the dough will be too stiff to roll.

To form the pot stickers, pinch off a tablespoon-sized piece of dough and roll it out into a circle about 3 inches in diameter. If you can, try rolling the edges a touch thinner than the center, so when you pleat them together, they don't get too thick.

Place a tablespoon of filling in the center of dough. Moisten the edge halfway around with water, then fold the dough over to form a half moon shape.

To seal, form 5 or 6 small pleats along the edge and press together, using your thumb and forefinger. Repeat this procedure with the remaining dough and filling.

Heat several tablespoons of oil in a wok (or non stick pan) over medium heat, swirling the wok so the oil coats the bottom surface. Gently lay enough pot stickers in a circular pattern to cover the bottom of the wok—it's OK if they slightly touch one another. Cook until the bottoms just begin to turn pale golden, 2 to 3 minutes. Pour in ½ cup of water, cover the wok, and let the pot stickers steam for 7 to 8 minutes. Remove the lid and continue cooking until the remaining water cooks off, about 1 to 2 minutes more. The pot sticker bottoms will be golden brown. Remove the cooked pot stickers, add a little more oil to the wok, and repeat until all they are all cooked.

To make the dipping sauce, combine all the ingredients in a small bowl. Serve with the hot pot stickers.

GRANDMA'S POCKMARKED TOFU (MA PO TOFU)

According to Chinese lore, this dish was invented by a pockmarked widow from Chengdu, the capital of Szechuan province, whose spicy, numbingly hot tofu dish became famous throughout the land. The heat from this dish typically comes from several sources—fiery heat from chilies and chili oil, numbing heat (*ma la*) from Szechuan peppercorns, and a savory spice from hot broad bean paste. Like many Chinese dishes, the small amount of meat relative to the amount of tofu used is deliberate—the pork serves more as a flavoring, and the tofu really has a chance to shine. Adjust the amount of chilies, chili oil, and peppercorns according to your taste.

SERVES 4 TO 6

¾ POUND GROUND PORK

2 TEASPOONS SHAO-HSING WINE OR
   DRY SHERRY

1 TEASPOON LIGHT SOY SAUCE

1 TEASPOON DARK SOY SAUCE

1 TEASPOON SESAME OIL

2 TABLESPOONS CORNSTARCH, DIVIDED

2 TABLESPOONS VEGETABLE OIL

1 OR 2 FRESH RED CHILIES, SLICED

1 OR 2 TABLESPOONS CHILI OIL

4 CLOVES GARLIC, FINELY MINCED

3 SCALLIONS, FINELY MINCED

30 OUNCES (3 PACKAGES) SOFT TOFU,
   DRAINED AND CUT INTO ½-INCH CUBES

3 HEAPING TABLESPOONS HOT
   BROAD BEAN SAUCE

1 TABLESPOON SZECHUAN PEPPERCORNS,
   TOASTED AND GROUND

TO SERVE:
STEAMED RICE

In a large bowl, mix the ground pork, wine, light and dark soy sauces, sesame oil, and 1 tablespoon of the cornstarch. Set aside to marinate for 20 minutes.

In a large wok, heat the vegetable oil, chilies, and chili oil over medium-high heat for 1 minute. Add the garlic and scallions and stir-fry for another minute to allow the flavor to release into the oil. Add the pork mixture, crumbling it with your spatula so the pieces of meat become small and pebbly. Take your time—this is an important step for the final texture of the dish, and you want to do a thorough job. Cook the pork until it is no longer pink, 5 to 6 minutes.

Gently, so as not to break up the pieces, add the tofu to the wok and heat through. Add the broad bean sauce and peppercorns, then toss gently, making sure the sauce coats all the tofu and pork evenly. Dissolve the remaining tablespoon of cornstarch in 2 tablespoons of water and add it to the wok. When the liquid bubbles up and thickens, remove the wok from the heat.

Serve immediately with steamed rice.

CHICKEN

RECIPES

KUNG PAO CHICKEN

Homemade kung pao chicken is a favorite on nights when I want a slightly less greasy version of this Chinese restaurant staple. This dish is a snap to put together; it's guaranteed to hit your dinner table faster than speed dial takeout delivery. To save even more time, marinate the chicken the night before, for a meal you can whip up in less than fifteen minutes the next day.

SERVES 2

1 POUND SKINLESS, BONELESS CHICKEN
   (PREFERABLY THIGH MEAT), CUT INTO
   BITE-SIZE PIECES
1 TABLESPOON SHAO-HSING WINE OR DRY SHERRY
1 TEASPOON DARK SOY SAUCE
1 TABLESPOON LIGHT SOY SAUCE
1½ TEASPOONS SESAME OIL
1½ TABLESPOONS CORNSTARCH
1½ TABLESPOONS SUGAR
2 TO 3 HEAPING TABLESPOONS CHINESE
   HOT CHILI SAUCE
3 TABLESPOONS VEGETABLE OR PEANUT OIL

5 CLOVES GARLIC, SMASHED BUT LEFT WHOLE
10 SCALLIONS, CUT INTO BITE-SIZE PIECES
5 TO 15 DRIED RED CHILIES
2 TABLESPOONS CHINESE BLACK OR RICE VINEGAR
¼ CUP ROASTED, SALTED PEANUTS
¼ TEASPOON GROUND SZECHUAN
   PEPPERCORNS (OPTIONAL)

TO SERVE:
STEAMED JASMINE RICE

Put the chicken in a large bowl, then add the wine, dark and light soy sauces, sesame oil, cornstarch, sugar, and chili sauce to taste. Stir the chicken until well-coated and marinate for at least 30 minutes in the refrigerator. (The marinating chicken can be covered and refrigerated up to one day ahead.)

Heat the vegetable oil in a wok over high heat. Add the garlic, scallions, and chilies to taste, and stir for 1 minute to 1½ minutes to flavor the oil. (They will start to blister and brown at this point.) Add the chicken, and cook until opaque and cooked through, 6 to 7 minutes. To test for doneness, cut one piece of chicken in half; it should no longer be pink in the middle.

Add the vinegar, peanuts, and peppercorns and toss to distribute evenly. Serve over steamed jasmine rice.

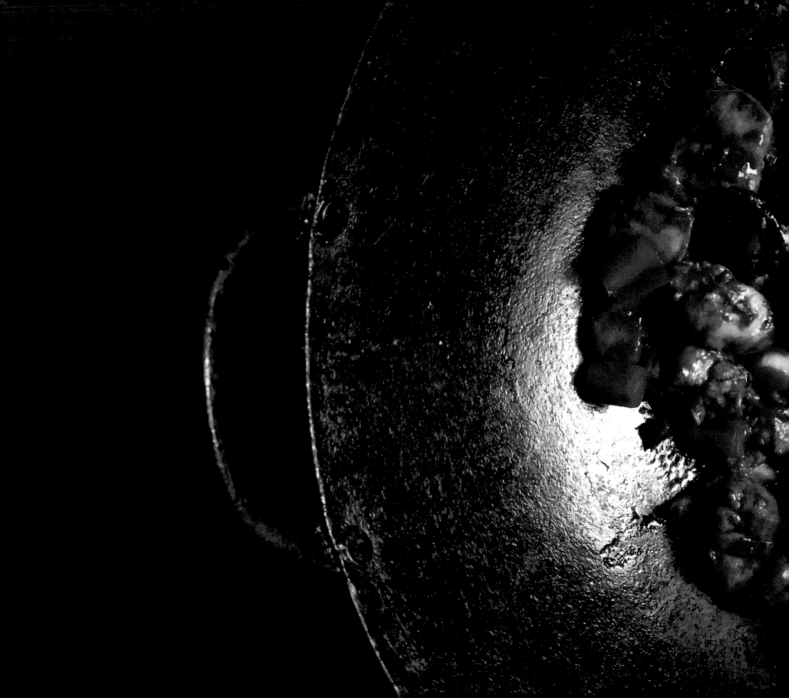

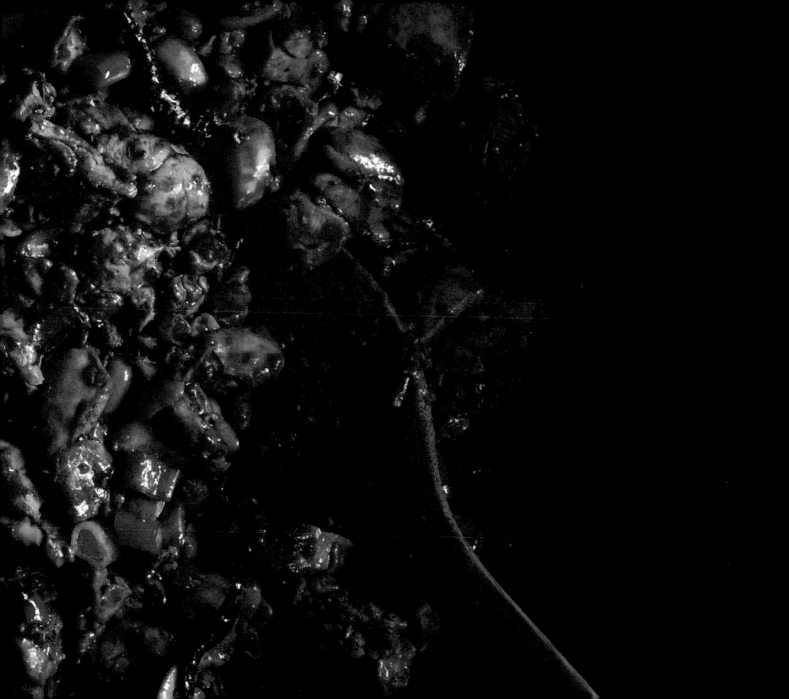

EASY CHICKEN CHOW MEIN

Aromatics like ginger, scallions, and garlic elevate this everyday stir-fried noodle dish into something sublime. You can find dried Chinese noodles in the Asian section of any grocery store. Note: Chinese noodles cook up faster than their Western counterparts. To prevent overcooking, boil them for a few minutes less than the package directions state, because you'll be stir-frying the boiled noodles for a few more minutes later on in the recipe.

SERVES 2 TO 4

1 POUND BONELESS, SKINLESS CHICKEN
   (PREFERABLY DARK MEAT), THINLY SLICED

1½ TABLESPOONS LIGHT SOY SAUCE

1 TABLESPOON SHAO-HSING WINE OR DRY SHERRY

2 TEASPOONS ASIAN CHILI SAUCE (OPTIONAL)

1 TEASPOON CORNSTARCH

2½ TEASPOONS SESAME OIL, DIVIDED

3 TABLESPOONS OYSTER SAUCE

¼ CUP CHICKEN STOCK

7 OUNCES DRIED CHINESE WHEAT NOODLES

5 TABLESPOONS VEGETABLE OIL, DIVIDED

4 OUNCES (1 CUP) FRESH SHIITAKE OR
   OTHER MUSHROOMS (PREFERABLY
   SHIITAKE), FINELY SLICED

4 SCALLIONS, THINLY SLICED

1 TABLESPOON FRESH GINGER, FINELY MINCED

1 TABLESPOON FRESH GARLIC, FINELY MINCED

1 SMALL BUNCH CHIVES, CUT INTO 3-INCH PIECES

In a large bowl, toss together the chicken, soy sauce, wine, chili sauce, cornstarch, and 1 teaspoon of the sesame oil to thoroughly combine. Let the chicken marinate for 20 minutes.

In another bowl, combine the oyster sauce and chicken stock and set aside.

Bring a pot of salted water to a boil. Cook the noodles for 2 minutes less than the package directions and drain.

In a wok, heat 2 tablespoons of the vegetable oil over high heat. Stir-fry the chicken until 75 percent cooked through, 4 to 5 minutes. Remove from the wok and set aside.

Heat the remaining 3 tablespoons of oil in the wok. Add the mushrooms, scallions, ginger, and garlic and stir-fry for 3 to 4 minutes. Add the chicken, chives, and noodles and stir-fry for another 2 minutes. Pour the oyster sauce and chicken mixture over the mixture and toss to thoroughly coat. Just before serving, drizzle with the remaining 1½ teaspoons sesame oil.

CHICKEN AND ANDOUILLE SAUSAGE GUMBO

This slow-simmered, one-wok meal is just the thing to serve up on a blustery fall or winter evening. Rich and hearty, chock-full of chicken, andouille sausage, and shrimp, this gumbo is perfect over steamed rice. It's also great for making ahead—the flavors develop after sitting overnight in the fridge, rendering leftovers even more delicious.

SERVES 6

2 TABLESPOONS VEGETABLE OIL

1½ POUND BONELESS CHICKEN (PREFERABLY DARK MEAT)

KOSHER SALT AND FRESHLY GROUND BLACK PEPPER

5 TABLESPOONS BUTTER

⅓ CUP ALL-PURPOSE FLOUR

1 LARGE SWEET ONION, DICED

6 CLOVES GARLIC, SMASHED

1 GREEN BELL PEPPER, CHOPPED

3 STALKS CELERY, DICED

4 CUPS CHICKEN STOCK

3 TABLESPOONS WORCESTERSHIRE SAUCE

1 POUND ANDOUILLE SAUSAGE, CUT INTO ¼-INCH SLICES

2 CUPS FRESH OR FROZEN SLICED OKRA

4 SCALLIONS, FINELY MINCED

ONE 12-OUNCE CAN CRUSHED TOMATOES

2 BAY LEAVES

¼ TEASPOON CAYENNE

¾ POUND LARGE SHRIMP, PEELED AND DEVEINED

TO SERVE:

STEAMED RICE, LEMON WEDGES, HOT SAUCE, CHOPPED PARSLEY (OPTIONAL)

Heat the oil in a wok over medium-high heat.
Season the chicken lightly with salt and pepper
and brown the meat for about 3 minutes.
Remove the chicken from the wok and set aside.

Melt the butter in the wok and stir in the flour.
Cook, stirring, until the paste takes on a reddish-
brown color, about 10 minutes. This is the
roux, the base for the gumbo. To the roux, add
the onion, garlic, pepper, and celery. Cook the
vegetables until softened, about 5 minutes.

Add the browned chicken, stock, Worcestershire,
sausage, frozen okra, scallions, tomatoes, bay
leaves, and cayenne to taste to the wok. Reduce
the heat to medium and cook, covered, for 2½
hours, stirring occasionally. Just before serving,
add the shrimp and stir into the gumbo until
cooked through, about 8 minutes. Remove and
discard the bay leaves.

Dish up the gumbo over steamed rice and serve
with lemon, hot sauce, and parsley.

STIR-FRIED CHICKEN LETTUCE WRAPS WITH PEANUT SAUCE

These little lettuce wraps are so much fun to eat—just spoon a little sticky rice onto a leaf, top with a delicious stir-fried mix of garlicky chicken with hoisin sauce, and dip each jade parcel into the tangy-sweet peanut sauce.

SERVES 2 TO 4

FOR THE PEANUT SAUCE:
⅓ CUP CREAMY PEANUT BUTTER
2 TABLESPOONS HOT WATER
1 TABLESPOON LIGHT SOY SAUCE
1 TABLESPOON RICE VINEGAR
1 TEASPOON SUGAR (OR SLIGHTLY MORE)
1 TEASPOON SRIRACHA OR OTHER
 ASIAN CHILI SAUCE
1 TEASPOON SESAME OIL

FOR THE CHICKEN:
1 POUND GROUND CHICKEN
2 TABLESPOONS HOISIN SAUCE
1 TEASPOON LIGHT SOY SAUCE
⅛ TEASPOON FRESHLY GROUND WHITE PEPPER,
 OR ¼ TEASPOON BLACK PEPPER
2 TEASPOONS CORNSTARCH
3 TABLESPOONS VEGETABLE OIL
2 SHALLOTS, FINELY MINCED
3 CLOVES GARLIC, FINELY MINCED
¾ CUP WATER CHESTNUTS, FINELY DICED

2 OUNCES (½ CUP) FRESH SHIITAKE MUSHROOMS,
 STEMMED AND SLICED
BUTTER LETTUCE LEAVES FOR WRAPPING
1½ CUPS COOKED STICKY RICE

To make the sauce, in a medium bowl, stir together all the ingredients for the sauce and set aside.

To make the chicken, in a large bowl, combine the chicken, hoisin sauce, soy sauce, pepper, and cornstarch. Let the chicken marinate for 20 minutes.

In a wok, combine the oil, shallots, and garlic. Over medium-high heat cook until the shallots and garlic turn golden brown and fragrant, about 2 to 3 minutes. Add the chicken, water chestnuts, and mushrooms. Cook, stirring, until the chicken and vegetables are cooked through, 6 to 7 minutes.

Serve the chicken with the lettuce, sticky rice, and dipping sauce.

WEEKEND COQ AU VIN

Coq au vin evolved from a favorite dish of French peasants, who invented this luscious, hearty stew when their roosters grew too old for much else. After hours of cooking at a low temperature, the once tough and stringy meat became soft and meltingly tender, while the red wine sauce reduced and thickened into a full-bodied, glossy liquid perfect for spooning over wide noodles or sopping up with crusty bread. Though not many of us have roosters scratching around in our backyards anymore, this dish has stood the test of time. When I feel that first lick of winter frost in the air, I like to make up a nice pot of this coq au vin and invite some of our best friends over for dinner. What makes this particular recipe extra special is that you begin by roasting the vegetables and the chicken for a short time to caramelize them, which adds another dimension of flavor.

SERVES 4

2 MEDIUM CARROTS, CUT INTO ¼-INCH COINS

2 MEDIUM PARSNIPS, CUT INTO ¼-INCH COINS

2 STALKS CELERY, CUT INTO ½-INCH PIECES

2 TABLESPOONS OLIVE OIL

ONE 4½-POUND ROASTING CHICKEN,
　CUT INTO 8 PIECES

KOSHER SALT AND FRESHLY GROUND
　BLACK PEPPER

3 CUPS FULL-BODIED RED WINE

½ CUP PORT WINE

2 CUPS DARK CHICKEN STOCK
　(PREFERABLY HOMEMADE)

2 BAY LEAVES

4 CLOVES GARLIC, SMASHED BUT
　LEFT WHOLE

8 SPRIGS FRESH THYME

1 TEASPOON CHOPPED FRESH MARJORAM,
　OR ½ TEASPOON DRIED

4 SLICES THICK-CUT BACON,
　CUT INTO ¼-INCH PIECES

2 TABLESPOONS BUTTER

2 TABLESPOONS FLOUR

1½ CUPS (ABOUT 4 OUNCES)
　HALVED PEARL ONIONS

8 OUNCES (2½ CUPS) CREMINI MUSHROOMS,
　QUARTERED

TO SERVE:

CRUSTY BREAD OR WIDE NOODLES

Preheat the oven to 425 degrees F.

Distribute the carrots, parsnips, and celery in an even layer on a parchment-lined baking sheet. Drizzle the vegetables with the oil and place the chicken on top of the vegetables. Season everything lightly with salt and pepper. Roast until the vegetables are softened and slightly browned and the chicken is lightly browned, about 25 minutes.

Transfer the roasted vegetables and chicken to a wok. Pour in the wine, port, and stock, add the bay leaves, garlic, thyme, and marjoram, and season lightly with salt and pepper. (Make sure the chicken is submerged in the liquid.) Bring the chicken and vegetables to a boil over high heat, then reduce the heat to medium-low. Cover the wok and simmer until the chicken is falling-off-the-bone tender, 2 to 2½ hours. Skim off any surface fat and discard. Strain out the vegetables, thyme sprigs, garlic, and bay leaves and discard. Remove the chicken from the braising liquid with a slotted spoon and set it aside.

Simmer the sauce over medium heat until slightly reduced, about 15 to 20 minutes. Return the chicken to the wok, with the heat on medium-low.

Meanwhile, in a skillet over medium-high heat, sauté the bacon until crisp. Add the butter to the skillet with the bacon. Add the pearl onions and mushrooms and cook until the vegetables caramelize, 7 to 8 minutes. Add the flour to the skillet, and cook everything together for 1 more minute to get rid of the raw flour taste. Add the mixture to the wok and stir into the chicken. The flour will thicken up the sauce considerably.

Serve the coq au vin in large bowls with hunks of crusty bread for dipping, or spoon it over wide noodles.

OLD-FASHIONED SOUTHERN BUTTERMILK FRIED CHICKEN

Whether hot out of the fryer or served cold at a picnic, this fried chicken remains crisp on the outside, juicy on the inside, and amazingly delicious. The secret is an overnight soak in buttermilk, which tenderizes the meat, so be sure to allow for the extra time. The breading is spicy with garlic, onion, cayenne, and paprika—a combination that will have everyone reaching for seconds.

SERVES 4

FOR THE CHICKEN:
ONE 4-POUND CHICKEN
1 QUART BUTTERMILK, DIVIDED
6 CLOVES GARLIC, SMASHED
1 LARGE LEMON, HALVED
2 BAY LEAVES
2 TABLESPOONS KOSHER SALT
1 TABLESPOON FRESHLY GROUND BLACK PEPPER

FOR THE BREADING:
4 CUPS ALL-PURPOSE FLOUR
3 TABLESPOONS GARLIC POWDER
3 TABLESPOONS ONION POWDER
1 TABLESPOON CAYENNE
1 TABLESPOON SMOKED PAPRIKA
2 TABLESPOONS KOSHER SALT
1 TABLESPOON FRESHLY GROUND BLACK PEPPER
VEGETABLE OIL FOR FRYING (PREFERABLY PEANUT)

To make the chicken, cut it into 8 pieces: two breasts, two thighs, two legs, and two wings. In a large pot or mixing bowl, combine 3 cups of the buttermilk, garlic, lemon, bay leaves, salt, and pepper. Submerge the chicken pieces in the buttermilk mixture. Cover and set the bowl in the refrigerator overnight, turning the chicken pieces before bed to ensure thorough saturation.

When ready to proceed with cooking, transfer the chicken from the buttermilk to a bowl. To make the breading, combine all the ingredients in another bowl. Divide the breading mixture into 2 shallow dishes. Pour the remaining cup of buttermilk into a third dish.

Dip each piece of chicken into the first dish of flour, then into the buttermilk, and then into the second dish of flour, shaking off the excess flour and letting the excess buttermilk drip off. Set the pieces on a rack. Make sure each piece is coated evenly, with as much breading as possible adhering to the meat.

In a wok, heat several inches of oil to 350 degrees F, measuring with a deep-fry thermometer. Carefully lower 2 to 3 pieces of chicken into the oil. The oil temperature should drop to about 325 degrees F—if not, lower the heat a bit. Monitor the oil so that it hovers around 325 degrees F as you fry the chicken, turning the pieces midway through. The cooking time should be 11 to 12 minutes for each batch of chicken thighs, legs, and breasts. The wings will cook in about 8 to 9 minutes. Cut into a piece of chicken to check doneness—there should be no pink, and juices should run clear.

Transfer the cooked chicken to a wire rack to cool slightly before serving.

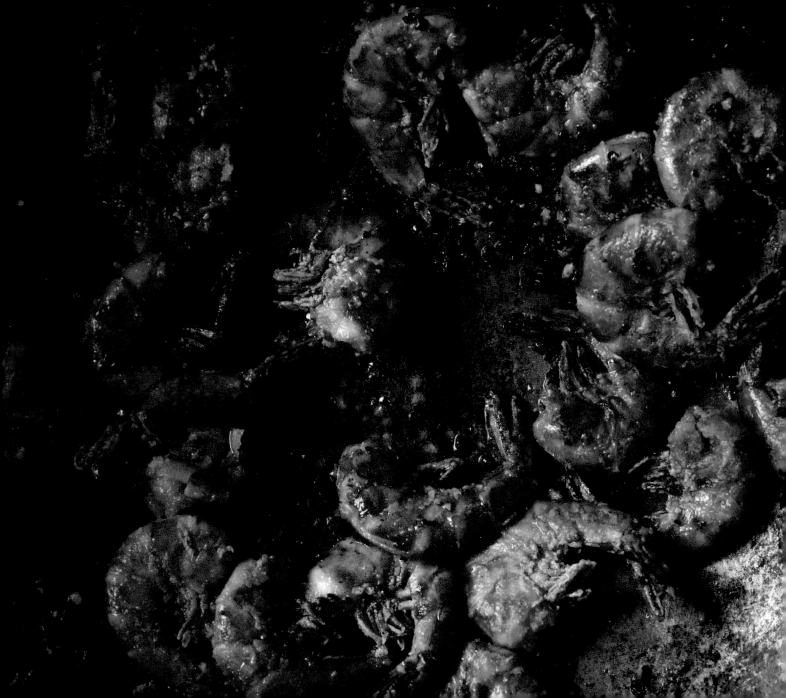

SEAFOOD

RECIPES

BIG 'N' MESSY OYSTER PO' BOYS

Packed full of plump, garlicky-crisp fried oysters and creamy slaw, these po' boys are a five-napkin meal that'll leave you with a satisfied smile. For a twist on this New Orleans classic, feel free to toss a few shrimp in the same breading.

MAKES 2 LARGE SANDWICHES

FOR THE SLAW:
⅓ CUP MAYONNAISE
2 TABLESPOONS CREOLE MUSTARD
1 TABLESPOON PREPARED HORSERADISH
1 TABLESPOON FRESHLY SQUEEZED LEMON JUICE
TABASCO SAUCE
1 CUP PACKED SHREDDED RED CABBAGE
KOSHER SALT AND FRESHLY GROUND
   BLACK PEPPER

FOR THE EGG WASH:
1 EGG, BEATEN
⅔ CUP MILK
½ TEASPOON CAYENNE

FOR THE BREADING:
¾ CUP CORNMEAL
1 CUP ALL-PURPOSE FLOUR
2 TABLESPOONS GARLIC POWDER
1 TABLESPOON KOSHER SALT
1 TEASPOON FRESHLY GROUND BLACK PEPPER
1 POUND MEDIUM OYSTERS, SHUCKED
VEGETABLE OIL FOR FRYING

TO SERVE:
2 HOAGIE ROLLS, SPLIT, BUTTERED, AND
   LIGHTLY TOASTED
1 TOMATO, THINLY SLICED
LEMON WEDGES AND HOT SAUCE (OPTIONAL)

To make the slaw, combine the mayonnaise, mustard, horseradish, lemon juice, and Tabasco sauce to taste in a small bowl. Put the cabbage in a separate bowl and dress with as much of the mayonnaise mixture as desired. Cover and refrigerate as you prepare the oysters.

To make the egg wash, combine the ingredients in a shallow dish.

To make the breading, put all the ingredients to a resealable plastic bag and shake to combine. Soak the oysters in the egg wash for 5 minutes. Drain off the excess, then put the oysters in the plastic bag with the breading. Seal the bag and shake until the oysters are completely coated.

In a wok, heat several inches of oil to 375 degrees F, measuring with a deep-fry thermometer. Remove the oysters from the bag and fry in batches until golden, about 3 minutes per batch, setting them aside on paper towels to drain.

Dress each roll with some slaw and sliced tomato. Divide the oysters between the 2 sandwiches. Serve with a squeeze of lemon and/or hot sauce.

BEER-BATTERED FISH WITH EASY GARLIC AIOLI

With a light, crisp batter and an easy, whisk-together aioli for dipping, this fish is guaranteed to be some of the best you've ever tasted. My favorite beverage to accompany this special treat is—surprise!—bubbly champagne.

SERVES 4

FOR THE GARLIC AIOLI:
¾ CUP MAYONNAISE
3 CLOVES GARLIC, FINELY MINCED
3 TABLESPOONS FRESHLY SQUEEZED
   LEMON JUICE (FROM 1 LARGE LEMON)
1½ TABLESPOONS CHOPPED FRESH PARSLEY

FOR THE BATTER:
2 CUPS ALL-PURPOSE FLOUR
1 TABLESPOON SMOKED PAPRIKA
2 TABLESPOONS GARLIC POWDER
½ TEASPOON CAYENNE
1 EGG
ONE 12-OUNCE BOTTLE BEER

2 POUNDS COD, CUT INTO 4-OUNCE FILLETS
KOSHER SALT AND FRESHLY GROUND
   BLACK PEPPER
VEGETABLE OIL FOR FRYING

TO SERVE:
LEMON WEDGES AND/OR MALT VINEGAR

To make the garlic aioli, whisk all the ingredients together in a bowl. Cover and refrigerate for at least 30 minutes before serving.

To make the beer-battered fish, whisk together all the ingredients for the batter in a large bowl. Cover and refrigerate for at least 30 minutes and up to 2 hours.

Pat the fish dry with a paper towel. Season both sides to taste with salt and pepper.

In a wok, heat several inches of oil to 365 degrees F, measuring with a deep-fry thermometer.

Dip a fillet into the batter, then carefully slide it into the hot oil. Repeat with a few more fillets, but do not overcrowd the oil. (The temperature of the oil will dip down a little, to about 350 degrees F at this point.) Fry the first batch until it turns golden brown, about 5 minutes. Drain the pieces and set aside. Repeat with the remaining fillets.

Serve with lemon, malt vinegar, and the garlic aioli.

STIR-FRIED ASIAN CHILI CRAB

Enrobed in an addictive tangy-sweet-spicy sauce and fragrant with ginger, garlic, and scallions, this chili crab is sure to become a hit in your household. The sauce is particularly delicious over steamed rice or noodles. For extra heat, punch it up with a diced serrano pepper.

SERVES 4

FOR THE SAUCE:
¼ CUP KETCHUP
2 TABLESPOONS SRIRACHA (OR MORE)
1 TABLESPOON SOY SAUCE
2 TABLESPOONS OYSTER SAUCE
2 TABLESPOONS SUGAR
2 TABLESPOONS SHAO-HSING WINE OR
 DRY SHERRY
1 TABLESPOON TAMARIND PASTE
⅓ CUP WATER

FOR THE CRAB:
TWO 2½-POUND DUNGENESS CRABS
¼ CUP VEGETABLE OIL
5 CLOVES MINCED GARLIC

3 SCALLIONS, FINELY CHOPPED
1½-INCH-PIECE GINGER, PEELED AND MINCED
1 SERRANO PEPPER (OPTIONAL)
2 TABLESPOONS CORNSTARCH,
 DISSOLVED IN ¼ CUP WATER
1 EGG, BEATEN

TO SERVE:
STEAMED RICE
NOODLES

To make the sauce, in a large bowl, combine all the ingredients. Set aside.

To make the crab, remove and discard the top shell, keeping the meaty legs and claws with shell intact, then clean the gills. Cut the crab lengthwise in half; then cut each half into 3 pieces of roughly equivalent size.

STEAMED SALMON WITH FENNEL AND DILL

During the Copper River salmon season, this refreshing dish makes an appearance once a week. The moist salmon is a wonderful foil for the citrusy fennel slaw, rounded out with creamy feta and crunchy pistachios. Serve it with wild rice or a baked sweet potato for a light and healthful meal. Or, if you prefer, this figure-friendly meal leaves you plenty of room for some post-dinner ice cream!

SERVES 4

FOR THE SALMON:

TWO 1-POUND WILD SALMON FILLETS,
   CUT INTO 4 EQUAL PORTIONS
KOSHER SALT AND FRESHLY GROUND
   BLACK PEPPER
3 TABLESPOONS DRY WHITE WINE

FOR THE FENNEL AND DILL SALAD:

⅓ CUP OLIVE OIL
¼ CUP FRESHLY SQUEEZED LEMON JUICE (FROM 2
   MEDIUM LEMONS)
1 TABLESPOON HONEY
2 MEDIUM FENNEL BULBS, TRIMMED AND
   SHAVED INTO PAPER-THIN SLICES
⅓ CUP SHELLED PISTACHIOS
½ CUP CRUMBLED FETA OR GOAT CHEESE
3 TABLESPOONS FRESH DILL, FINELY CHOPPED
KOSHER SALT AND FRESHLY GROUND
   BLACK PEPPER

To make the salmon, put the fish in a shallow, heatproof dish or bowl. Season with salt and pepper to taste and pour the wine over it.

Pour about an inch of water into the bottom of a wok and add a steamer rack. Bring the water to a boil over high heat, then set the bowl of fish on the rack, lowering the heat to medium to maintain a simmer. Cover and steam the fish for 10 to 12 minutes. Monitor the water level, adding more if needed to ensure that the wok doesn't go dry. Test for doneness with a fork—the fish should be moist and just beginning to flake.

To make the salad, in a bowl, whisk together the oil, lemon, and honey. Drizzle as much of the dressing as desired over the fennel, then toss with the pistachios, cheese, and dill. Season to taste with salt and pepper.

To serve, place a piece of salmon on each plate alongside a portion of the salad.

SEAFOOD PAELLA

Many home cooks don't own a dedicated pan for making paella, but in a pinch, a well-seasoned wok works beautifully. This Spanish rice dish is flavored with a base made with olive oil, tomatoes, garlic, peppers, onions, and saffron, then absorbs the delicious juices from the seafood, chicken, and chorizo sausage as it simmers away. Ideal for feeding a crowd, this impressive recipe looks much more labor intensive than it really is.

SERVES 8

½ CUP EXTRA-VIRGIN OLIVE OIL, DIVIDED

1 POUND BONELESS CHICKEN THIGHS,
CUT INTO BITE-SIZE PIECES

1 SPANISH ONION, DICED

1 CUP TOMATO PURÉE

4 CLOVES GARLIC, MINCED

6 PIQUILLO PEPPERS, MINCED

1 TEASPOON PAPRIKA

1 TEASPOON SAFFRON THREADS

KOSHER SALT AND FRESHLY GROUND
BLACK PEPPER

2 CUPS RICE (PREFERABLY CALASPARRA OR BOMBA)

4 CUPS SHELLFISH OR CHICKEN BROTH

1 CUP DRY WHITE WINE

1 POUND SPANISH CHORIZO SAUSAGE,
CUT INTO ¼-INCH SLICES

½ POUND LARGE SHRIMP

½ POUND BAY SCALLOPS

1 POUND MUSSELS OR CLAMS

½ POUND SQUID

¾ CUP PEAS, FRESH OR FROZEN

TO SERVE:

LEMON WEDGES

Heat 3 tablespoons of the olive oil in a wok over medium-high heat. Brown the chicken in the oil, about 3 minutes per side. Add the remaining 5 tablespoons of olive oil and the onion and sauté until golden, about 5 minutes. Add the tomato purée, garlic, peppers, and paprika. Lightly crush the saffron threads, then stir them into the vegetables. Season everything lightly with salt and pepper. Let the vegetables to cook down for 2 to 3 minutes, then stir in the rice.

Pour in the broth and wine. Tuck in the chorizo pieces and stir the paella. Partially cover the wok and cook over medium heat, stirring occasionally (about every 3 to 4 minutes), until the chicken and chorizo are cooked through, 20 to 25 minutes. (Watch the rice so that the bottom doesn't scorch, adjusting the heat to medium-low if necessary.)

Uncover the wok and scatter the shrimp, scallops, mussels, and squid over the rice. Stir in the peas. Cover the wok completely and allow the paella to cook over medium heat for another 8 to 10 minutes, stirring occasionally. At this point, check the rice for doneness—you should be close. When the rice and seafood are cooked through, serve with lemon wedges.

CRISPY SALT-AND-PEPPER SHRIMP

With shrimp encased in a crisp batter, then stir-fried again in a heady mix of Szechuan peppercorns, five-spice powder, garlic, and chiles, this dish is more fragrant than full-on spicy. Deep-frying with the shell on protects the tender shrimp meat from the heat, so it reaches your dinner table super moist and tender each and every time. Note: Some intrepid diners enjoy eating the shrimp with its fried shell on; others discard it before eating.

SERVES 2 TO 4

- **1 POUND LARGE SHRIMP, HEADS REMOVED AND DEVEINED, SHELLS ON**
- **1 TABLESPOON SHAO-HSING WINE OR DRY SHERRY**
- **2 TEASPOONS LIGHT SOY SAUCE**
- **½ TEASPOON SESAME OIL**
- **1½ TEASPOON KOSHER SALT, DIVIDED**
- **¼ CUP CORNSTARCH**
- **VEGETABLE OIL FOR FRYING**
- **1 SERRANO CHILI, DICED**
- **4 CLOVES GARLIC, FINELY DICED**
- **½ TEASPOON SZECHUAN PEPPERCORNS, ROASTED AND GROUND**
- **¼ TEASPOON CHINESE FIVE-SPICE POWDER**

Rinse the shrimp and pat dry. In a large bowl, combine the shrimp with the wine, soy sauce, sesame oil, and ½ teaspoon salt. Let the shrimp marinate for 15 to 20 minutes.

Drain the shrimp and pat dry; discard the marinade. Toss the shrimp in the cornstarch.

Heat several inches of vegetable oil in a wok over medium-high heat. Carefully drop the shrimp into the oil in batches. The shrimp should cook through in 50 to 60 seconds (the shells will turn bright pink). Remove them with a slotted spoon and drain on paper towels.

Discard all but 2 tablespoons of the oil in the wok. Add the salt, chili, garlic, peppercorn, five-spice powder, and 1 teaspoon salt to the oil, still over medium-high heat. Stir the seasonings into the oil for 1 minute. Return the shrimp to the wok and toss to combine for 30 seconds. Serve immediately.

MY FAVORITE PASTA, WITH ANCHOVIES, GARLIC, AND CHILIES

The first time I ate this classic Italian combination of flavors was at one of my favorite Seattle restaurants, Anchovies & Olives. It was one of those late-night dinners that I enjoyed over candlelight, in a dim and bustling restaurant filled with the sounds of hungry patrons giddy over the incredible, soul-satisfying bowls of pasta coming from the kitchen. The heat of chilies, combined with the deep saltiness of anchovies and punctuated by bright lemon, is irresistible. The crunch of panko and the slivers of Parmesan just push this dish over the top. I created this recipe so that I'd never be more than fifteen minutes away from this incredible dish, and I hope you enjoy it as much as I do.

SERVES 4

12 OUNCES BUCATINI PASTA OR SPAGHETTI

½ CUP OLIVE OIL

14 OIL-PACKED ANCHOVY FILETS, PLUS ONE
   TABLESPOON ANCHOVY OIL

6 CLOVES GARLIC, COARSELY CHOPPED

⅔ CUP PARSLEY, FINELY CHOPPED

½ TEASPOON CRUSHED RED PEPPER FLAKES
   (OR MORE)

½ CUP PANKO

JUICE OF ½ LEMON

½ CUP GRATED PARMESAN (PREFERABLY
   PARMIGIANO-REGGIANO)

KOSHER SALT AND FRESHLY GROUND
   BLACK PEPPER

Bring a large pot of salted water to a boil. Cook the pasta according to the package directions and drain.

In a wok over medium-low heat, heat the olive oil and anchovies, stirring until the anchovies dissolve, about 2 to 3 minutes. Add the garlic, parsley, and red pepper flakes to taste and stir until the oil is infused with their flavor, 4 to 5 minutes.

Add the pasta directly to the wok. Toss to coat with the sauce, then sprinkle with the panko.

To serve, squeeze in the lemon juice and top with Parmesan at the table. Season to taste with salt and pepper.

CLASSIC SHRIMP-AND-EGG FRIED RICE

The secret to this popular staple dish is using day-old long-grain rice. "Leftover" rice, refrigerated overnight after cooking, is drier than fresh-cooked rice, so it fries up with that elusive restaurant-cooked texture. A whisper of ginger in this classic shrimp-and-egg combination makes it extra special—and tastier than takeout.

SERVES 2

½ POUND MEDIUM-SIZE SHRIMP,
   PEELED AND DEVEINED
½ TEASPOON KOSHER SALT
1 TEASPOON CORNSTARCH
4 TABLESPOONS VEGETABLE OIL, DIVIDED
2 TEASPOONS FRESHLY GRATED GINGER
3 SCALLIONS, FINELY CHOPPED
3 EGGS, BEATEN
3 CUPS DAY-OLD COOKED LONG-GRAIN WHITE RICE
½ CUP FROZEN PEAS
2 TO 3 TEASPOONS SOY SAUCE
1 TEASPOON SESAME OIL

In a small bowl, toss the shrimp, salt, and cornstarch, and let sit for 10 minutes.

Heat 2 tablespoons of the oil in a wok over high heat. Fry the shrimp on both sides until they just begin to turn opaque, about 1 minute per side. Remove the shrimp from the wok, and set aside.

Add the remaining 2 tablespoons of oil to the wok. Fry the ginger, scallions, and eggs until the eggs are still runny but just beginning to set—less than 1 minute. Immediately add the rice and cook, stirring, so that the egg breaks up into small pieces that cling to the rice.

Add the frozen peas and soy sauce to taste. Continuing cooking until the rice is sizzling hot. Add the shrimp and cook for 1 more minute. Drizzle the sesame oil over the top and serve.

MISO-STEAMED BLACK COD

Fish novices, rejoice: if you've been reluctant to try cooking fish at home, this easy recipe is a great jumping-off point. Black cod's rich texture makes it difficult to overcook, especially when steamed. Steaming is both a very healthful *and* a flavorful way to enjoy fish, as it allows a certain purity of flavor to shine through. Note: Plan ahead, as the fish must marinate overnight before cooking.

SERVES 4

FOR THE MARINADE:

⅓ CUP SAKE

2 TABLESPOONS MIRIN (SWEET RICE WINE)

¼ CUP WHITE MISO PASTE

¼ CUP SUGAR

1 TABLESPOON LIGHT SOY SAUCE

ONE 1-INCH-PIECE FRESH GINGER,
   FINELY SLIVERED

¼ CUP SCALLIONS, FINELY MINCED

FOUR 6-OUNCE BLACK COD FILLETS

TO SERVE:

STEAMED RICE

1 TEASPOON SESAME OIL

To make the marinade, combine all the ingredients for the marinade in a wok over medium heat and stir until the sugar is dissolved. Let the marinade cool, then pour it into a resealable plastic bag. Put the cod fillets in the bag and seal it. Refrigerate, turning the bag over once before you head off to bed.

To steam the fish, remove it from the pouch and discard the marinade. Pour a few inches of water into the bottom of a wok and set a rack or bamboo steamer over the water. Cover the wok and bring the water to a boil over high heat. Put the fish on the rack and steam until it is opaque and cooked through, 10 to 15 minutes. Monitor the level of water in the wok, adding more as needed to ensure that it doesn't go dry. You'll know the fish is done when it flakes with little resistance.

To serve, arrange the fish on a bed of steamed rice and drizzle with the sesame oil.

VEGETARIAN

RECIPES

LEMONY ASPARAGUS RISOTTO

When the frost dissipates and springtime ushers in fat, flavorful stalks of asparagus at your farmers' market, try this lemony risotto. Enriched with white wine and Parmesan, this dish easily stands alone as a lovely meal—or, topped with seared scallops, a romantic one. The last-minute addition of mascarpone cheese guarantees that this risotto will be the creamiest, dreamiest you've ever eaten.

SERVES 4 TO 6

5 CUPS CHICKEN OR VEGETABLE BROTH

1 CUP DRY WHITE WINE

¼ CUP (½ STICK) BUTTER

1 TABLESPOON OLIVE OIL

2 LARGE SHALLOTS, CHOPPED

2 CUPS ARBORIO RICE

1 CUP ASPARAGUS TIPS, CUT INTO 1-INCH PIECES

1 CUP GRATED PARMESAN

¼ CUP MASCARPONE CHEESE

ZEST OF 1 LARGE LEMON

3 TABLESPOONS FRESHLY SQUEEZED
   LEMON JUICE

KOSHER SALT AND FRESHLY GROUND
   BLACK PEPPER

In a stockpot, combine the broth and the wine. Bring to a boil over high heat, then lower the heat to medium-low to keep the liquid at a simmer.

In a wok over medium heat, melt the butter and add the olive oil. Sauté the shallots until golden, about 4 minutes. Add the rice and stir, gently "toasting" it for 2 minutes. Add the asparagus and 1½ cups of the simmering liquid. Cook, stirring, until the liquid is almost completely absorbed by the rice.

Add the remaining liquid a ladleful at a time and continue stirring until the rice is cooked through and tender and the liquid is completely absorbed, about 35 minutes.

Stir in the Parmesan, mascarpone, and lemon zest and juice. Season to taste with salt and pepper and serve.

SCALLION PANCAKES

Unlike many Asian grandmothers, my maternal grandma (my Po Po) did not have an extensive repertoire of dishes. Marrying into a considerably wealthy family meant a kitchen full of cooks who made sure a variety of dishes—farm-fresh stir-fries, steamed whole fishes, and slow-braised meats—outfitted the dinner table each evening. One of the few dishes she taught me was this Scallion Pancakes recipe, when I was a girl of about ten years old. I still remember her gnarled hands curled over mine as we rolled out the soft rounds of dough together.

SERVES 4

2 CUPS ALL-PURPOSE FLOUR
¾ CUP HOT BUT NOT BOILING WATER
½ TEASPOONS KOSHER SALT
½ CUP SHORTENING OR VEGETABLE OIL, DIVIDED
½ CUP SCALLIONS, FINELY CHOPPED, DIVIDED
VEGETABLE OIL FOR FRYING

In a mixing bowl, stir together the flour, water, and salt until it forms a sticky dough.

On a lightly floured surface, knead the dough until it becomes smooth, soft, and elastic, about 10 minutes. Place the dough in a covered bowl, or seal it in a plastic bag for 30 minutes, and allow it to rest.

Divide the dough into 4 equal pieces. Roll out the first piece of dough into a roughly circular form, about ⅛-inch-thick. Spread the surface of the dough with 2 tablespoons shortening. Sprinkle 2 tablespoons of the scallions over the shortening. Starting from one end, roll the dough into a cigar shape as compactly as possible. Coil the dough like a cinnamon bun, so that the shortening and scallions are encased in the dough. Roll out the dough flat again into a circular pancake, about ¼-inch-thick. Repeat with the remaining pieces of dough.

Heat 2 or 3 tablespoons of oil in a wok over medium-high heat. Place 1 pancake into the wok, and lower the heat to medium. Fry the pancake until golden brown, about 3 minutes, then flip. Continue cooking the other side until golden brown. Set the finished pancake aside. Add a little more oil to the pan, and when hot, repeat frying the remaining dough until all the pancakes are cooked.

Cut the pancakes into wedges and serve.

THE CREAMIEST MAC 'N' CHEESE

This ultra-creamy mac 'n' cheese is like velvet on the tongue. A four-cheese blend ensures plenty of gooeyness, and a crispy panko topping offers a lovely textural contrast. Cuddle up with a big bowl of this on any wintry evening to chase away the cold-weather blues.

SERVES 4

FOR THE BREAD CRUMB TOPPING:
2 TABLESPOONS BUTTER
¾ CUP PANKO

FOR THE MAC 'N' CHEESE:
3 CUPS ELBOW MACARONI
3 TABLESPOONS BUTTER
3 TABLESPOONS ALL-PURPOSE FLOUR
1 ½ CUPS MILK
¾ CUP MASCARPONE CHEESE
KOSHER SALT AND FRESHLY GROUND
  BLACK PEPPER
¼ TEASPOON CAYENNE PEPPER
½ TEASPOON DRY MUSTARD
2 ½ CUPS GRATED SHARP CHEDDAR CHEESE
1 CUP GRATED GRUYÈRE
⅔ CUP GRATED PARMESAN

Cook the macaroni according to package directions and drain. Set aside.

To make the topping, melt the butter in a small saucepan over medium–high heat. Add the panko and toast until golden brown, about 3 minutes. Set aside.

To make the mac 'n' cheese, in a wok melt the butter over medium heat. Stir the flour into the butter until it forms a paste. Add the milk and mascarpone and cook, stirring, until the sauce thickens, 4 to 5 minutes.

Season the sauce with salt and pepper to taste, cayenne, and dry mustard. Add the cheddar, Gruyère, and Parmesan and cook, stirring, until melted. Stir in the macaroni. To serve, divide the mac 'n' cheese among 4 serving bowls and sprinkle with the toasted panko.

CREAMY ROASTED CAULIFLOWER AND WHITE CHEDDAR SOUP

Roasting cauliflower renders it tender and sweet beyond compare. Coupled with a touch of cream and a few handfuls of shredded cheese, this humble vegetable will yield one of the loveliest wintry soups you've ever tasted.

SERVES 4

1 MEDIUM HEAD CAULIFLOWER, CUT INTO FLORETS
3 TABLESPOONS VEGETABLE OIL, DIVIDED
KOSHER SALT AND FRESHLY GROUND
   BLACK PEPPER
1 TABLESPOON BUTTER
3 CLOVES GARLIC, SMASHED
6 SPRIGS FRESH THYME
1 MEDIUM SWEET ONION, DICED
3 CUPS VEGETABLE BROTH (PREFERABLY
   HOMEMADE)
2 CUPS SHREDDED WHITE CHEDDAR CHEESE
1 CUP HALF-AND-HALF

TO SERVE:
CRUSTY, BUTTERED BREAD

Preheat the oven to 425 degrees F.

In a medium bowl, toss the cauliflower florets with 2 tablespoons oil and season to taste with salt and pepper. Place the florets on a baking sheet, then roast the cauliflower until tender and lightly golden, about 20 to 25 minutes.

Heat the remaining tablespoon of oil and butter in a wok over medium heat. Add the garlic, thyme, and onion and cook until the onions are softened and golden, about 10 minutes.

Pour the broth into the wok and add the cauliflower. Simmer the cauliflower in the broth for 30 minutes on medium heat, adjusting the heat to medium-low if necessary.

Purée the soup with an immersion blender (or ladle into a regular blender) until smooth. Pour the soup back into the wok. Stir in the cheese and half-and-half until the cheese as melted.

Season to taste with salt and pepper and serve with crusty, buttered bread.

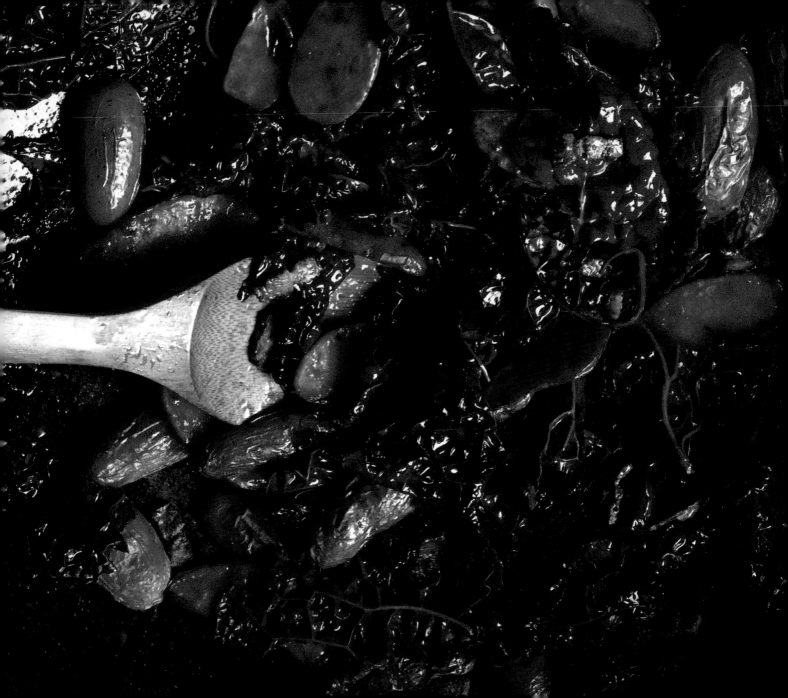

RECIPES

PANCETTA AND SWEET POTATO CROQUETTES

It's easy to see why it's so hard to stop eating these sweet-and-savory croquettes. Flecked with pancetta and fresh sage, held together with creamy sweet potato, they are a little too easy to pop into your mouth—one after the other! The fall flavors in this side dish make it a wonderful alternative to the standard sweet potato casserole at your next holiday meal, or a great weeknight dress-up for your go-to roast chicken. Note: You need to chill the mixture for several hours before you fry the croquettes.

SERVES 6

4 OUNCES PANCETTA OR BACON,
  CUT INTO ¼-INCH PIECES
3 CUPS COOKED, MASHED YAM OR
  SWEET POTATO
2 TABLESPOONS DARK BROWN SUGAR
2 TEASPOONS FRESH SAGE, FINELY CHOPPED
KOSHER SALT AND FRESHLY GROUND
  BLACK PEPPER
1 EGG

FOR THE BREADING:
2 EGGS
2½ CUPS PANKO
VEGETABLE OIL FOR DEEP-FRYING
  (PREFERABLY PEANUT)

Fry the pancetta in a wok over medium heat until crisp and golden. Scoop out the pancetta with a slotted spoon and drain in a sieve over a mixing bowl. Reserve 2 tablespoons of the drippings and discard the rest.

To the drippings, add the yam, pancetta, brown sugar, sage, and salt and pepper to taste. Stir in the egg. Refrigerate the mixture for at least 4 hours before proceeding.

After the mixture has chilled, scoop out heaping tablespoonfuls and roll them between your hands to form 1-inch balls. Place the balls on a lined baking sheet.

To make the breading, in a shallow dish, beat the eggs until thoroughly liquid. Place the panko in a separate dish.

Roll each ball first in the panko, then in the egg wash, then again in the panko, shaking off the excess panko and letting the excess egg wash drip off. Repeat until all the croquettes are coated.

In a wok, heat 2 inches of oil over medium-high heat. Once the oil is hot, lower the heat to medium, or until the oil just maintains a simmer. Fry the croquettes in batches until golden brown, 1 or 2 minutes per side. Remove the croquettes with a slotted spoon and drain on paper towels. Serve immediately.

THE EASIEST, SINGLE-FRY FRENCH FRY

Call us crazy, but we've discovered a way to produce a crisp, fluffy, golden French fry, without the need for multiple soaks in water or messy double fryings at different temperatures. Best of all? Frying them in your wok speeds along the wok-seasoning process; the large amount of oil used helps the wok develop that coveted shiny-slick, jet-black patina that only the most treasured vessels see in their lifetime. With only three ingredients, this recipe is easy enough for the busiest of weeknights. (If you have duck fat on hand for frying, these fries will taste even better!)

SERVES 2 TO 4

**2 LARGE RUSSET POTATOES, UNPEELED, CUT INTO
¼-BY-¼-INCH STRIPS OF EQUAL LENGTH**
1 QUART PEANUT OIL OR DUCK FAT
KOSHER SALT

TO SERVE:
**KETCHUP, GARLIC AIOLI (PAGE 75), OR
(OUR FAVORITE) CHEESE CURDS AND
GRAVY TO MAKE *POUTINE***

Rinse the potatoes under cold water and pat dry with a towel.

Pour the oil into a wok and submerge the potato strips in the cold oil. Bring the oil to a rolling boil over medium-high heat, which should take about 4 to 5 minutes. Lower the heat to medium to retain a boil and continue to cook, without stirring, for about 20 to 22 minutes, or just until the potatoes are lightly golden.

If any fries are sticking to the wok at this point, stir to unstick them. Continue to cook until the fries are golden brown, another 3 to 5 minutes.

To check for doneness, remove one fry from the oil and cut it in half—the interior should be cooked through and fluffy. When the fries are done, remove them from the oil with a frying strainer, season lightly with salt, and drain on paper towels.

Serve with bowls of ketchup or aioli for dipping, or top the fries with gravy and crumbled cheese curds for *poutine*.

STIR-FRIED GARLICKY GREEN BEANS

In this classic Chinese recipe, long beans are stir-fried in the wok until their skins start to blister and pucker, rendering them incredibly soft and delicious. The beans are then bathed in a flavorful sauce made with garlic, ginger, soy sauce, and chilies, rounded out with just a touch of sugar. Note: After washing the beans, it's important to dry them thoroughly before frying; excess moisture will make the hot oil splatter.

SERVES 2 TO 4

4 TABLESPOONS VEGETABLE OIL
   (PREFERABLY PEANUT), DIVIDED
1 POUND CHINESE LONG BEANS OR GREEN
   BEANS, CUT INTO 3-INCH PIECES
5 CLOVES GARLIC, FINELY CHOPPED
1 TEASPOON FRESH GINGER, FINELY CHOPPED
4 TO 6 DRIED RED CHILIES
2 TEASPOONS SHAO-HSING WINE OR DRY SHERRY
2 TABLESPOONS LIGHT SOY SAUCE
1 TEASPOON SUGAR
2 TEASPOONS CHINESE CHILI OIL
KOSHER SALT
¼ TEASPOON GROUND SZECHUAN
   PEPPERCORNS (OPTIONAL)
1 TEASPOON SESAME OIL

Heat 3 tablespoons of the oil in a wok over high heat. Add the beans and cook until they soften and their skin starts to blister, about 5 to 7 minutes. Transfer the beans to a dish.

Lower the heat to medium and add the remaining tablespoon of oil to the wok. Add the garlic, ginger, and red chilies to taste and cook until fragrant, about 1 minute. Stir in the wine, soy sauce, sugar, and chili oil. Add the beans and toss to thoroughly coat with the sauce. Season to taste with salt and add the Szechuan pepper. Remove from the heat, drizzle with the sesame oil, and serve immediately.

STIR-FRIED SUMMER CORN, BACON, AND BROCCOLI RABE

When fresh summer corn is at its peak, try this easy five-ingredient (salt and pepper notwithstanding) recipe. The natural sugars in corn caramelize beautifully in the wok, making it taste even sweeter.

SERVES 4

2 TABLESPOONS VEGETABLE OIL
1 BUNCH BROCCOLI RABE
4 SLICES THICK-CUT BACON, DICED
3 TABLESPOONS BUTTER
4 MEDIUM EARS SWEET CORN,
   KERNELS CUT FROM THE COBS
KOSHER SALT AND FRESHLY GROUND
   BLACK PEPPER

Heat the oil in a wok over high heat. Add the broccoli rabe and cook, stirring occasionally, until the greens soften and slightly sear, about 5 minutes. Remove the broccoli and set aside.

Wipe the wok clean (being careful with the hot surface) or use another wok, over high heat, to cook the bacon until crisp, 3 to 4 minutes. Remove the bacon from the wok with a slotted spoon, leaving the drippings in the wok.

To the drippings, add the butter and corn kernels. Cook the corn over high heat until the kernels just turn golden brown in areas, 3 to 4 minutes. Return the broccoli rabe and the bacon to the wok and toss to combine. Season to taste with salt and pepper and serve.

HOLIDAY CREAMED SPINACH WITH PARMESAN

Made with fresh baby spinach, this holiday staple gets a bit of a makeover with a cheesy twist. Serve this creamy side dish with a standing rib roast, a roast turkey or goose, or a festive ham.

SERVES 6

2 POUNDS FRESH SPINACH

¼ CUP (½ STICK) BUTTER

1 LARGE SWEET ONION, FINELY CHOPPED

3 CLOVES GARLIC, SMASHED

¼ CUP ALL-PURPOSE FLOUR

1 CUP HEAVY CREAM

1 CUP WHOLE MILK

PINCH OF FRESHLY GRATED NUTMEG

⅔ CUP GRATED PARMESAN (PREFERABLY
   PARMIGIANO-REGGIANO)

KOSHER SALT AND FRESHLY GROUND
   BLACK PEPPER

In a wok over medium heat, cook the spinach until just wilted. Drain the spinach and set aside. Discard any liquid left in the wok.

Heat the butter over medium–high heat. Add the onion and garlic and sauté until golden brown, 6 to 7 minutes. Add the flour and cook, stirring, for 1 minute. Add the cream, milk, and nutmeg. Cook the sauce, stirring, just until it bubbles and thickens. Lower the heat to medium.

Stir in the spinach and the Parmesan. Season to taste with salt and pepper and serve.

MARSALA-GLAZED MUSHROOMS

Draping a few spoonfuls of these succulent mushrooms over roast chicken or steak transforms a regular weeknight meal into a real event. Browned in butter and accented with golden shallot and fresh thyme, they are also fantastic tucked inside a hot baked potato.

SERVES 2 TO 4

¼ CUP (½ STICK) BUTTER

1 MEDIUM SHALLOT, FINELY DICED

1¼ POUNDS (5 CUPS) FRESH MUSHROOMS (PREFERABLY PORCINI), CUT INTO ¼-INCH SLICES

¼ CUP MARSALA WINE

½ TEASPOON CHOPPED FRESH THYME

KOSHER SALT AND FRESHLY GROUND BLACK PEPPER

Melt the butter in a wok over medium heat. Add the shallot and sauté until golden brown, about 5 minutes. Increase the heat to medium-high and add the mushrooms. Cook, stirring occasionally, until the mushrooms soften, 6 to 7 minutes.

Pour in the marsala, add the thyme, and toss until thoroughly combined. Continue cooking until the marsala bubbles and reduces by a half. Season to taste with salt and pepper and serve immediately.

ROASTED FINGERLING POTATOES WITH BACON AND GREENS

Golden-brown fingerling potatoes are sautéed with crisp bacon and greens, then tossed in a light and tangy vinaigrette. This side dish is so hearty and delicious, you just might be tempted to make a meal of it.

SERVES 4

1 POUND FINGERLING POTATOES, HALVED

2 TABLESPOONS DUCK FAT OR OLIVE OIL

KOSHER SALT AND FRESHLY GROUND
  BLACK PEPPER

5 SLICES THICK-CUT BACON, DICED

1 TABLESPOON OLIVE OIL

1 BUNCH KALE, STEMS AND TOUGH RIBS
  REMOVED AND LEAVES CHOPPED

FOR THE VINAIGRETTE:

2 TABLESPOONS OLIVE OIL

3 TABLESPOONS CHAMPAGNE VINEGAR

1 TABLESPOON DIJON MUSTARD

1 TABLESPOON DARK BROWN SUGAR

Preheat the oven to 400 degrees F. Toss the potatoes with the duck fat and spread them out on a baking sheet. Season lightly with salt and pepper. Roast in the oven until golden, about 25 minutes, stirring midway to ensure even browning. Turn off the heat and leave the potatoes in the oven until you're ready to proceed.

Meanwhile, in a wok over medium-high heat, cook the bacon until crisp, 4 to 5 minutes. Remove the bacon from the wok with a slotted spoon and set aside. Add the olive oil to the bacon drippings. Cook the kale in the wok over medium-high heat until softened, 6 to 7 minutes. Turn off the heat and return the potatoes and the bacon to the wok.

To make the vinaigrette, in a small bowl, whisk together all the ingredients. Drizzle the vinaigrette over the potato mixture and toss to thoroughly coat. Taste and adjust the seasoning before serving.

SLOW-COOKED COLLARD GREENS WITH HAM HOCK GRAVY

A staple on every proper Southern table, these slow-cooked greens take on the flavor of smoky ham hocks after simmering together for several hours. A thick wedge of corn bread or hot buttered biscuits are all you need to ensure that not a drop of that oniony, hammy gravy goes to waste.

SERVES 4 TO 6

3 TABLESPOONS VEGETABLE OIL
1 LARGE SWEET ONION, THINLY SLICED
3 TABLESPOONS ALL-PURPOSE FLOUR
3 BAY LEAVES
6 CLOVES GARLIC, FINELY MINCED
5½ CUPS CHICKEN STOCK
2 POUNDS BONE-IN SMOKED HAM HOCKS
   (ASK THE BUTCHER TO CUT EACH HOCK
   INTO 4 PIECES)
2 BUNCHES COLLARD GREENS, TOUGH STEMS
   REMOVED, CUT INTO BITE-SIZE PIECES
KOSHER SALT AND PLENTY OF FRESHLY
   GROUND BLACK PEPPER
RED PEPPER FLAKES

TO SERVE:
CORN BREAD OR BISCUITS

Heat the oil in a wok over medium-high heat until hot, about 1 minute. Add the onions and cook until they are golden brown, 10 to 12 minutes. Add the flour and stir until it is dissolved. (This forms the base for the gravy.)

Add the bay leaves, garlic, stock, ham hocks, collard greens, and salt, pepper, and pepper flakes to taste. Reduce heat to medium-low and partially cover the wok. Simmer, stirring occasionally, until the greens are cooked down, the ham is falling off the bone, and the gravy cooks down and thickens, at least 3 hours (and up to 4 hours for better flavor).

Serve with your favorite corn bread or hot buttered biscuits.

JALAPEÑO AND FRESH CORN HUSH PUPPIES

Juicy with fresh corn and dotted with spicy jalapeños, these hush puppies fry up light and golden—a perfect accompaniment to Slow-Cooked Collard Greens with Ham Hock Gravy (page 116) and Old-Fashioned Southern Buttermilk Fried Chicken (page 66).

SERVES 6 TO 8

1 CUP YELLOW CORNMEAL

1¼ CUPS ALL-PURPOSE FLOUR

¾ CUP FRESH CORN KERNELS (FROM ONE LARGE EAR OF CORN)

1 MEDIUM JALAPEÑO, SEEDED AND DICED

¼ CUP SCALLIONS, FINELY CHOPPED

3 TABLESPOONS SUGAR

2 TEASPOONS KOSHER SALT

1 TEASPOON FRESHLY GROUND BLACK PEPPER

3 TABLESPOONS BACON FAT OR MELTED BUTTER

1½ TEASPOONS BAKING POWDER

2 EGGS, BEATEN

1 CUP BUTTERMILK

VEGETABLE OIL FOR FRYING

In a large mixing bowl, gently stir together all the ingredients. (Do not overmix, as this will create dense, tough hush puppies!) Cover the bowl and refrigerate for at least 4 hours (and up to one day) until the batter is thoroughly chilled.

Preheat the oven to 250 degrees F. In a wok, heat a few inches of vegetable oil to 325 degrees F, measuring with a deep-fry thermometer. Using 2 teaspoons, scoop the batter into the hot oil, 1 heaping teaspoonful at a time, taking care not to overcrowd the wok. Fry the hush puppies until golden, turning occasionally, about 2 minutes per side.

With a slotted spoon, remove the hush puppies from the hot oil and drain over paper towels. Transfer them to a baking sheet to keep warm in the oven as you fry the remaining hush puppies. Serve hot, and season lightly with salt before serving.

DESSERT

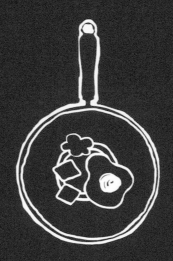

RECIPES

COCONUT MANGO PARFAITS

Need a simple, low-fuss dessert for a casual backyard barbecue? These delicious tropical parfaits are just the ticket–make the custard the night before, and you can assemble the parfaits moments before serving.

SERVES 4

FOR THE COCONUT CUSTARD:
2 TABLESPOONS CORNSTARCH
1¼ CUPS HEAVY CREAM, DIVIDED
1 TEASPOON VANILLA EXTRACT
¼ CUP SUGAR
¼ CUP (½ STICK) UNSALTED BUTTER
1¼ CUPS SWEETENED FLAKED COCONUT
⅓ CUP SOUR CREAM

12 TO 16 GINGERSNAP OR SHORTBREAD
   COOKIES, CRUMBLED
1 LARGE, RIPE MANGO, PEELED, PITTED, AND DICED
2 TABLESPOONS CONFECTIONERS' SUGAR

To make the custard, in a small bowl, dissolve the cornstarch in 2 tablespoons of water.

In a wok over medium-high heat, combine ¾ cup of the cream and the vanilla, sugar, and butter. Add the cornstarch and cook, stirring with a wooden spoon, until the mixture begins to boil. Remove from the heat and stir in the coconut and sour cream. Transfer the mixture to a bowl and cover with plastic wrap. Refrigerate for at least 6 hours or overnight.

In 4 parfait glasses, layer the crumbled cookies evenly with the custard and mango. Use as many cookies as you'd like, depending on whether you prefer a lot of cookie crunch or just a little.

In a mixing bowl, using a wooden spoon or an electric mixer, beat the remaining ½ cup whipping cream with the confectioners' sugar. Top each parfait with some whipped cream and serve.

CHURROS CON CHOCOLATE

Biting into one of these light, airy doughnuts, tossed in cinnamon sugar and dunked into hot, rich chocolate sauce, is one of life's greatest pleasures. In Spain, they're typically served at roadside stands or coffee shops for breakfast, sometimes with a steaming cup of *café con leche* for dipping. No matter when or where you choose to enjoy them, these Churros Con Chocolate are not to be missed! If you don't have a *churrera* (a churro press, widely available for purchase online), simply pipe the churro dough into the hot oil with a star-tipped pastry bag or a heavy-duty resealable plastic bag with one corner cutoff.

SERVES 4

FOR THE CINNAMON SUGAR:
½ CUP SUGAR
1½ TEASPOONS GROUND CINNAMON

FOR THE CHURROS:
1 CUP WATER
⅓ CUP UNSALTED BUTTER
2 TABLESPOONS SUGAR
¼ TEASPOON KOSHER SALT
1 CUP ALL-PURPOSE FLOUR
3 EGGS
VEGETABLE OIL FOR FRYING
  (PREFERABLY PEANUT)

FOR THE CHOCOLATE SAUCE:
1 CUP WHOLE MILK
1 TABLESPOON CORNSTARCH
6 OUNCES DARK CHOCOLATE (PREFERABLY
  BITTERSWEET), FINELY CHOPPED

To make the cinnamon sugar, in a plate, thoroughly combine the ingredients. Set aside.

To make the *churro*'s batter, in a medium saucepan combine the water, butter, sugar, and salt. Cook over medium heat, stirring with a wooden spoon, until the butter has melted. Add the flour all at once, and continue to stir until the mixture forms a ball and begins to dry out, about 1 minute.

Remove the saucepan from the heat. Using a wooden spoon, or with an electric mixer on medium speed, beat in the eggs, one at a time, until the dough is smooth and well combined.

Spoon the batter into a *churrera*. In a wok, heat 3 inches of oil to 360 degrees F, measuring with a deep-fry thermometer. Pipe the churros in

batches directly into the oil, leaving room for them to cook and be turned easily. Fry until golden, turning the churros with a wooden spoon so that each side cooks thoroughly. Remove the churros with a slotted spoon and drain on paper towels. While the churros are still hot, toss them in the cinnamon sugar to cover, then place on a serving platter. Repeat this process with the remaining batter.

To make the chocolate sauce, in a saucepan heat the milk and cornstarch together over medium heat, stirring with a whisk. When the milk begins to steam, stir in the chocolate and whisk until it melts completely. Remove from the heat and pour into small cups to serve for dipping with the churros.

CANNOLI WITH CHOCOLATE CHIP RICOTTA FILLING

One of my fondest memories is walking through Little Italy in New York with my husband, munching our way through a big box of fresh, filled-to-order cannoli. It was our first time tasting this traditional Italian treat the way it was meant to be enjoyed—with the flaky, extra-crisp shells struggling to encase all that smooth, creamy ricotta and mascarpone filling. Note: Allow at least an hour for the cannoli dough to chill before frying. A pasta machine is ideal, but you can get good results with an ordinary rolling pin, too.

MAKES 12 TO 14 CANNOLI

FOR THE CANNOLI:

2 CUPS ALL-PURPOSE FLOUR

3 TABLESPOONS SUGAR

3 TABLESPOONS BUTTER OR LARD, MELTED

1 EGG, PLUS 2 YOLKS

⅓ CUP MARSALA WINE

2 TO 3 TABLESPOONS WATER

1 EGG WHITE, LIGHTLY BEATEN, FOR
  SEALING THE DOUGH

VEGETABLE OIL FOR FRYING
  (PREFERABLY PEANUT)

FOR THE FILLING:

1 CUP WHOLE-MILK RICOTTA, DRAINED

1 CUP MASCARPONE CHEESE

¼ CUP CONFECTIONERS' SUGAR, PLUS MORE FOR
  DUSTING (OPTIONAL)

1 TABLESPOON FRESHLY SQUEEZED LEMON JUICE

1½ TEASPOONS GRATED ORANGE ZEST (OPTIONAL)

¼ CUP PISTACHIOS, FINELY CHOPPED (OPTIONAL)

MINI CHOCOLATE CHIPS, FOR DIPPING

To make the cannoli, in a mixing bowl, combine the flour and sugar. Make a well in the center and pour in the melted butter, egg and yolks, marsala, and water. Mix with a fork until the mixture forms a stiff dough. Turn the dough out onto a lightly floured surface and knead until it becomes smooth and pliable, 5 to 6 minutes. (If the dough feels too dry to come together, add another tablespoon of water and continue kneading.)

Wrap the dough in plastic wrap and refrigerate for at least 1 hour before proceeding.

Once the dough is chilled, if you have a pasta machine, divide it in half and run each half through the machine several times until you reach the thinnest setting. If you do not have a pasta machine, simply roll out the dough on a lightly floured surface with a rolling pin until you get it as thin as possible without tearing.

Using a large glass or cookie cutter 4 to 5 inches in diameter, cut out circles in the dough. Roll the dough around cannoli tubes, sealing the overlapping edge with a bit of egg white.

In a wok, heat a few inches of oil to 360 degrees F, measuring with a deep-fry thermometer. Fry the shells on the tubes a few at a time, taking care not to overcrowd the wok. Turn the shells as they become golden brown, about 1 to 2 minutes, then drain them on paper towels. Repeat with the remaining dough. Set the shells aside to cool.

To make the filling, combine the ricotta, mascarpone, confectioners' sugar, lemon juice, orange zest, and pistachios in a mixing bowl using a wooden spoon or an electric mixer on medium speed, beat until combined, about 3 minutes. Chill the filling in the refrigerator.

When you're ready to serve, fill a pastry bag (or a heavy-duty resealable plastic bag with a corner cut) with the filling and pipe it gently into the cooled cannoli shells. (Once filled, cannoli begin to soften, so fill them only when you're ready to serve them.) Dip the ends in chocolate chips, dust with confectioners' sugar, and serve immediately.

STICKY TOFFEE PUDDING

"Pudding" was once a more general term for "dessert." In this variation on the classic English dessert, a moist, sticky date cake is enrobed with hot caramel. Steaming this pudding in a wok is a snap, and its scaled-down size makes it the ideal homey treat for two or four.

SERVES 2 TO 4

FOR THE PUDDING:
¾ CUP (ABOUT 4 OUNCES) PITTED DATES
   (PREFERABLY MEDJOOL), PACKED
1 CUP WATER
¾ TEASPOON BAKING SODA
3 TABLESPOONS UNSALTED BUTTER,
   PLUS 1 TABLESPOON FOR GREASING
½ CUP LIGHT BROWN SUGAR, PACKED
1 EGG
½ TEASPOON VANILLA EXTRACT
¼ TEASPOON KOSHER SALT
1 CUP ALL-PURPOSE FLOUR

FOR THE SAUCE:
½ CUP (1 STICK) UNSALTED BUTTER
¾ CUP DARK BROWN SUGAR, PACKED
½ CUP HEAVY CREAM
SMALL PINCH OF KOSHER SALT

In a wok, combine the dates and water. Bring the mixture to a boil over high heat, then lower the heat to medium to keep it at a simmer until the dates are softened, 4 to 5 minutes. Remove the wok from the heat and stir in the baking soda. (Don't be alarmed—the mixture will foam up, then the foam will subside.)

Grease a small, heatproof bowl or pan with the 1 tablespoon butter. In a mixing bowl, using a wooden spoon or an electric mixer on medium speed, cream together the 3 tablespoons butter and the brown sugar until fluffy, 3 to 4 minutes. Beat in the egg, vanilla, and salt. Add the flour in 2 portions, beating thoroughly after each addition. Finally, beat in the date mixture until just combined. Scrape the batter into the greased bowl.

Line a clean wok with a folded tea towel. Place the pudding bowl directly on the tea towel and add enough water to the wok to come about

1½ inches up the side of the bowl. Cover the bowl tightly with aluminum foil.

Cover the wok. Bring the water to a boil over high heat, then lower the heat to medium to keep it at a simmer. Monitor the water level, adding more if needed to ensure it remains 1 to 1½ inches up the side of the bowl. Steam the pudding until a skewer inserted in the center comes out mostly clean, with a few moist crumbs, 1 hour to 1 hour 15 minutes. Cover the cooked pudding while you make the sauce.

To make the sauce, combine the butter, brown sugar, and cream in a clean wok or saucepan. Bring the mixture to a boil over high heat, then lower the heat to medium. Stir the simmering sauce until it reduces, about 15 minutes. Stir in the salt. Serve the warm pudding in bowls and top with a generous ladleful of sauce.

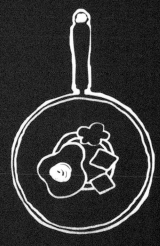

SUMMERTIME BLUEBERRIES WITH VANILLA CUSTARD SAUCE

When I was pregnant with my son, I had intense cravings for anything that involved dairy and fruit. This easy, rich, and pourable vanilla custard sauce transformed many a weeknight post-dinner snack of simple, sugared berries into something elegant—and it's perfectly suitable for company. The berries and custard sauce are also wonderful over a slice of golden pound cake. Note: Allow at least four hours for the custard sauce to chill before serving.

SERVES 4

FOR THE VANILLA CUSTARD SAUCE:
5 EGG YOLKS
2 CUPS HEAVY CREAM
1 VANILLA BEAN, HALVED LENGTHWISE AND
   SEEDS SCRAPED OUT OR 1½ TEASPOONS
   VANILLA EXTRACT
¼ CUP SUGAR

FOR THE BERRIES:
6 CUPS FRESH BLUEBERRIES
¼ CUP SUGAR
1 TABLESPOON COINTREAU (OPTIONAL)

To make the sauce, in a large bowl, lightly whisk together the yolks, cream, vanilla seeds, and sugar. Pour the mixture into a wok over medium heat. Add the vanilla to further infuse the custard.

With a wooden spoon, gently stir the mixture until it thickens, taking care that the custard doesn't boil or scorch. (You may have to adjust the heat to medium-low.) The custard should thicken enough to coat the back of the spoon after 10 to 12 minutes. (The custard will continue to thicken slightly as it cools.) Remove from the heat and discard the vanilla pod.

Pour the custard into a heatproof bowl or glass jar and refrigerate for at least 4 hours before serving.

To make the berries, stir them with the sugar and Cointreau in a large bowl, until the sugar is well incorporated. Let them rest on the counter for an hour or so, until the berries get nice and juicy.

To serve, divide the berries among 4 bowls and pour the vanilla custard over them.

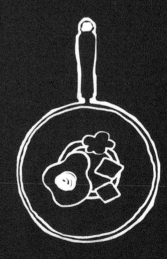

FRESH GINGER GINGERBREAD WITH LEMON CREAM

The robust flavors of this super-moist gingerbread pair beautifully with the sunny-yellow lemon cream, making this traditionally wintry cake suitable to enjoy year-round. This lemon cream is also lovely with buttery shortbread at teatime or with warm scones on a Sunday morning. Note: Allow time for the cream to chill for at least six hours before serving.

SERVES 8

FOR THE LEMON CREAM:
1 CUP SUGAR
1 TABLESPOON LEMON ZEST
4 EGGS
¾ CUP FRESHLY SQUEEZED LEMON JUICE
   (FROM 5 TO 6 LEMONS)
1 CUP (2 STICKS) UNSALTED BUTTER, AT ROOM
   TEMPERATURE, CUT INTO TABLESPOONS

FOR THE GINGERBREAD:
BUTTER FOR GREASING THE PAN
1 CUP MOLASSES
½ CUP SUGAR
¾ CUP VEGETABLE OIL
½ TEASPOON KOSHER SALT
1 TEASPOON GROUND GINGER
2 TABLESPOONS GRATED FRESH GINGERROOT

½ TEASPOON GROUND NUTMEG
1 TEASPOON CINNAMON
2 CUPS ALL-PURPOSE FLOUR
2 TEASPOONS BAKING SODA
1 CUP HOT WATER
2 EGGS

To make the lemon cream, line a clean wok with a folded tea towel. Place a medium heatproof mixing bowl on the towel and add enough water to the wok to come about 2 inches up the side of the bowl. Heat the water until it just comes to a boil on high heat, then lower the heat to medium to maintain a simmer.

In the bowl, whisk together the sugar, lemon zest, and eggs. Add the lemon juice and continue whisking until the mixture gets thick, 10 to 12 minutes. Gradually add the butter, a few tablespoons at a time, whisking each addition until thoroughly melted before adding more—this process should take about 5 minutes.

Remove the cream from the heat and lay a piece of plastic wrap over the surface to prevent a skin from forming. Refrigerate for at least 6 hours (or overnight) before serving.

To make the gingerbread, preheat the oven to 350 degrees F. Line the bottom of a 9-inch round, 3-inch deep cake pan with parchment paper. Lightly grease the sides of the pan with butter or vegetable oil.

In a large mixing bowl, stir together the molasses, sugar, oil, salt, gingers, nutmeg, and cinnamon. In a separate bowl, combine the flour and baking soda.

Stir the hot water into the molasses mixture. Add the flour in thirds, stirring until each addition is incorporated thoroughly. Finally, stir in the eggs.

Pour the batter into the prepared pan and smooth the top with a spatula.

Bake until a skewer inserted into the center comes out mostly clean, with a few moist crumbs, 55 to 60 minutes. Serve warm, or allow to cool—the cake is fantastic either way.

To serve, place slices on 8 serving plates and dollop with a few spoonfuls of lemon cream.

CLASSIC BREAD PUDDING WITH BOURBON CARAMEL SAUCE

When the temperature dips low, there isn't anything more comforting than a crackling fire and a big bowl of this pillowy bread pudding. Draped in buttery bourbon caramel, this soul-satisfying sweet will warm you to the core.

SERVES 6 TO 8

FOR THE BREAD PUDDING:
2 CUPS HEAVY CREAM
2 CUPS WHOLE MILK
4 EGGS
2 TABLESPOONS VANILLA EXTRACT
2 TEASPOONS GROUND CINNAMON
1½ CUPS SUGAR
½ TEASPOON KOSHER SALT
1 LOAF DAY-OLD FRENCH BREAD,
  CUBED (6 TO 7 CUPS)
2 TABLESPOONS SOFTENED BUTTER
  FOR GREASING

FOR THE BOURBON CARAMEL SAUCE:
1 CUP DARK BROWN SUGAR, PACKED
2 CUPS HEAVY CREAM
½ CUP (1 STICK) BUTTER
½ TEASPOON KOSHER SALT
1 TABLESPOON BOURBON

Preheat the oven to 350 degrees F.

In a large mixing bowl, whisk together the cream, milk, eggs, vanilla, cinnamon, sugar, and salt. Soak the bread in the mixture for about 20 minutes.

Grease a 9-by-13-inch casserole dish with the butter. Pour the bread and custard mixture into the dish. Bake until the pudding slightly puffs up and the edges turn a golden brown, 40 to 45 minutes.

To make the sauce, in a wok over medium-high heat, combine the brown sugar, cream, butter, and salt, stirring with a wooden spoon, until it just comes to a boil. Lower the heat to medium-low and continue stirring until the sauce thickens, about 15 to 20 minutes. Stir in the bourbon and remove the sauce from the heat.

Spoon the sauce generously over each dish of warm bread pudding and serve.

POACHED PEACHES WITH BUTTERMILK ICE CREAM

Although we here in Seattle may have to wait a little longer than the rest of the country to sink our teeth into plush, tree-ripened peaches each summer, this light and refreshing dessert makes the wait worthwhile. Poaching the peaches in prosecco and lightly sweetening them with honey really puts the emphasis on the fruit, so use the largest, sweetest peaches you can find. The tangy buttermilk ice cream is a delicious accompaniment—and is good on its own, too. Note: Both dishes should be started the day before serving.

SERVES 4

FOR THE PEACHES:
4 LARGE PEACHES
1 BOTTLE PROSECCO OR OTHER DRY SPARKLING WINE
2 TABLESPOONS SUGAR
¼ CUP HONEY
1 VANILLA BEAN, HALVED LENGTHWISE

FOR THE BUTTERMILK ICE CREAM:
2 CUPS HEAVY CREAM
2 CUPS BUTTERMILK
1 CUP SUGAR
1 VANILLA BEAN, HALVED LENGTHWISE, OR 1½ TEASPOONS VANILLA EXTRACT
8 EGG YOLKS

To make the peaches, have a bowl of ice water ready in the refrigerator. Fill a medium saucepan halfway with water. Bring the water to a boil over high heat. Add the peaches and lower the heat to medium. Simmer for 1 minute.

Remove the peaches with a slotted spoon and plunge them into the bowl of ice water. When the peaches feel cool to the touch, remove them from the water. With a knife, score the bottom of each peach with an X, then peel the skin away. The skins should slip off easily.

Halve the peaches and remove and discard the pits.

In a wok, combine the prosecco, sugar, honey, vanilla bean, and peaches. Over medium heat, simmer the peaches until tender, 10 to 12 minutes. Transfer the peaches to a bowl.

Heat the remaining poaching liquid over medium-high heat until it reduces by half. Pour the hot liquid over the peaches. Cover the bowl with plastic wrap and refrigerate for at least 6 hours before serving.

To make the ice cream, combine the cream, buttermilk, sugar, and vanilla bean (seeds and pod) in a clean wok. Heat the liquid, stirring, over medium-high heat until it steams. Do not let the mixture scorch or boil over.

In a large heatproof bowl, whisk together the egg yolks. Gradually ladle the hot liquid over the yolks in a slow stream, whisking steadily so the yolks warm up but do not cook. Return the mixture to the wok and cook, stirring, over medium heat until thickened, 10 to 12 minutes. The custard should be steaming hot but must

not boil. (You may have to adjust the heat to medium-low if it looks as if the mixture is getting too hot too quickly.)

Transfer the thickened custard base to a large heatproof bowl. Remove the vanilla pod and discard. Cover the bowl with plastic wrap and let the custard cure in the refrigerator overnight.

The next day, process the custard according to your ice cream maker manufacturer's instructions.

To serve, divide the peaches among 4 individual bowls. Place a generous scoop of ice cream on each, and drizzle with a few spoonfuls of the poaching liquid.

CINNAMON-SUGAR FRIED APPLE PIES

My (very Southern) friend Jenifer Ward introduced me to the wonders of fried pie a couple of years ago (her unique quince pie filling has gained her great renown in our circle). This Southern staple is, in my opinion, less tricky to make than a traditional baked pie, and possibly even tastier! With a crunchy, golden brown pastry and the familiar sweet-tart taste of cinnamon apple filling, these flaky, handheld beauties will be a hit at any holiday gathering. Jenifer stresses that the lean, biscuit-like dough is key—the pies will be too greasy if you use a regular pie crust recipe.

MAKES 6 FRIED PIES

FOR THE FILLING:

2 LARGE APPLES (PREFERABLY GRAVENSTEIN, GRANNY SMITH, OR PINK LADY), PEELED, COVERED, AND DICED INTO ½-INCH PIECES

⅓ CUP LIGHT BROWN SUGAR, PACKED

1 TABLESPOON FRESHLY SQUEEZED LEMON JUICE

½ TEASPOON GROUND CINNAMON

⅛ TEASPOON GROUND CLOVES

⅛ TEASPOON GROUND NUTMEG

2 TABLESPOONS BUTTER

FOR THE DOUGH:

2 CUPS ALL-PURPOSE FLOUR

1 TEASPOON KOSHER SALT

1 TABLESPOON SUGAR

½ CUP LARD OR SHORTENING

½ CUP MILK (AND UP TO 2 TABLESPOONS MORE, IF NEEDED)

4 CUPS VEGETABLE OIL FOR FRYING (PREFERABLY PEANUT)

SUGAR FOR DUSTING

To make the filling, combine the apples, brown sugar, lemon juice, cinnamon, cloves, and nutmeg in a wok over medium heat. Cook, stirring with a wooden spoon, until the apples soften, 10 to 15 minutes. Stir in the butter and set the filling aside to cool.

To make the dough, combine the flour, salt, and sugar in a large mixing bowl. Cut the lard into the flour mixture with a pastry blender or your fingertips until the fat is well incorporated and the mixture looks like coarse sand. (Unlike a traditional pie crust, with this one you don't want pea-size pieces of fat.)

Stir in the milk and gather and squeeze the dough together until it forms a ball. If the dough seems too dry, add the extra milk, a little at a time, and squeeze it together again until it forms a ball.

Divide the dough into 6 equal pieces and flatten each piece into a small disk with the heel of your hand. Roll out each piece on a lightly floured surface until it is about ⅛-inch thick and roughly 4 inches in diameter. Heap a large spoonful of filling in the center. Fold the dough over the filling and crimp the edges with a fork to seal. Repeat with the remaining dough and filling.

In a clean wok, heat the oil to 350 degrees F, measuring with a deep-fry thermometer. Fry the pies a few at a time (without crowding—4 is a good number) until golden on one side. Flip the pies with a spatula and continue frying until the other sides are golden. Drain the pies on paper towels and dust with sugar while still hot. Repeat with the remaining pies and serve warm.

INDEX

Note: Photographs are indicated by *italics*.

ABOUT THE AUTHOR

LORNA YEE is the coauthor of *The Newlywed Kitchen: Delicious Meals for Couples Cooking Together*, and food columnist at *Seattle* magazine. Born and raised in Vancouver, BC, she found love just over the border and made the move shortly after. She currently resides in Seattle with her husband, new baby, and their pampered dog. This is her second cookbook.